The Hidden Teacher

Also by Anthony P. Barber:

Common Threads: Investigating and Solving School Discipline
The Hidden Principalship: A Practical Handbook for New and Experienced Principals
Culture, Clichés, and Conversations: Improving Teacher-Administrator Relations

The Hidden Teacher

Not Only Surviving the System, But Thriving in It!

Anthony P. Barber

ROWMAN & LITTLEFIELD
Lanham • Boulder • New York • Toronto • Plymouth, UK

Published by Rowman & Littlefield
4501 Forbes Boulevard, Suite 200, Lanham, Maryland 20706
www.rowman.com

10 Thornbury Road, Plymouth PL6 7PP, United Kingdom

British Library Cataloguing in Publication Information Available

Library of Congress Cataloging-in-Publication Data

Library of Congress Cataloging-in-Publication Data Available

ISBN 978-1-4758-0869-8 (cloth : alk. paper) -- ISBN 978-1-4758-0870-4 (pbk. : alk. paper) -- ISBN 978-1-4758-0871-1 (electronic)

∞™ The paper used in this publication meets the minimum requirements of American National Standard for Information Sciences Permanence of Paper for Printed Library Materials, ANSI/NISO Z39.48-1992.

Printed in the United States of America

This book is dedicated to Brielle, our Angel of Hope.

"You can't touch what's inside . . . me."

Disclaimer

This text is offered solely as a guide and potential resource to and for educators who live and work in a constantly changing and dynamic environment. It is not intended to be and indeed is not an all-encompassing work that addresses each and every potential situation or issue that is or may be encountered in the realm of education. It does not provide a step-by-step, guaranteed manual for success via wooden application of the concepts, ideas, and suggestions presented herein. Instead, this is a rendering and distillation of information crafted by an educator that may be of use to other educators. The application of that information is wholly dependent upon the innumerable facts and circumstances and other intangible components that are part and parcel of each individual challenge or opportunity that may be presented in any individual situation.

Contents

Foreword

Education is a people business. In fact, it is *the* people business. Novice and veteran teachers alike attempt to balance the demands of the job, negotiating their relationships with not only the students and their parents, but also with their fellow teachers and administrators. Every teacher has experienced the promise and pitfalls that accompany the first few years of teaching.

The Hidden Teacher offers practical advice for many of the common problems faced by beginning (and experienced) teachers, dealing with the complex issues of power, control, and motivation. These issues of power and control constitute the "hidden" curriculum that must be mastered in order for teachers to experience success. Filled with practical advice and case studies, this book is a welcome and insightful addition to educational literature that reveals to the reader the systems that influence their ability to teach and lead. This book is a guide that helps teachers create rewarding connections with their students, parents, and colleagues.

Dr. Barber devotes chapters to many practical topics, using relatable stories and anecdotes to illustrate his points. With these stories, the author offers practical suggestions to help the reader find resolutions to common issues facing teachers, such as:

- A lesson in perspective: Human discretion and determining right and wrong
- All I do for this place: A teacher's sense of ownership
- What's the win: How to handle a school's special interest groups
- And many more!

I remember my own first years of teaching. I was hired the Friday before Labor Day because the school had secured a grant. My excitement was only outmatched by my fear of what was to come. Although I had a strong pedagogical knowledge base, it was the "stuff" they didn't teach you in school—how to deal with people—that taught me how much I still had to learn. I wish that I had had a resource to help me navigate those challenging waters. That's why *The Hidden Teacher* is perfect for teachers new to the profession, teachers new to a school, or teachers looking to revitalize their practice.

Dr. Barber brings his years of experience as a classroom teacher, subject area coordinator, assistant principal, principal, and Director of Teach-

ing and Learning to assist other educators in handling common chal-
lenges they face. His passion for the profession and his commitment to
the craft of teaching is inspiring. In *The Hidden Teacher*, he shares his
inspiration to help teachers when facing both common and complex issues.

Education is a people business. It is *the* people business. I invite you to
read, think, and improve your practice.

—Melissa Butler, EdD

Preface

An elderly woman peered from her living room window. "What's all that racket out there?" Her motivation stirred. She had become accustomed to certain "nice-lies" as she termed them. And one of her favorite flavors took the form of stillness. As her eyes came into focus, she noticed a blue car stuck in the chunky, white snow. "Snow in October?" she thought to herself. "Strange times."

The "racket" she had heard took the form of a young man pleading for assistance. "Anybody!" He called. "Anyone?" Quickly, she positioned herself behind her purple drapes to conceal her existence. "This guy could be a crazy person," she murmured aloud. "That's all I need." Likewise, she justified her thoughts through recognition. She tuned into the six o'clock news; society was a mess. It's just easier to become an empty window rather than a cracked one.

After a few tense moments, the calling ceased. She felt relieved; yet, the hush tweaked her curiosity. Knowing she might regret the impulse, she decided to take a second glance. Finally, with a deep breath, she pushed forward to the empty window.

"Ah!" She grasped and returned to the safety of the drapes. The young man was standing inches from her window.

"Could you give me a hand, please? My car is stuck, and I am late for work." Her heart raced as she heard his plea. What to do? What to do? He called again, "Miss. Miss."

Unfortunately for the elderly woman, she had come to realize that this stranger was not going away. She knew she was the only person on her block at this time of day. Maybe he knew that too. Maybe he had been watching, waiting. In any event, the situation had presented itself. She must face the window. With a Herculean effort, she placed herself in his sights.

"Miss." He said to her. She did not reply. "Miss?" He tagged again. And still, she could not seem to muster a response. At this moment, the man placed his lips one inch away from the window and let out an enormous breath. In turn, the window fogged so much that she could no longer see the man. Her fear pitched. Maybe this was it?

Suddenly, without warning, she saw his finger against the window craft the letter P. This was followed in succession by other letters until the word became clear . . . PLEASE!

As the inscription finished, she caught a glimpse of his hazel eyes through the E's. He was cold, tired. He could have been her son. He was someone's son. He was.

With an uncontrollable force, she pointed for him to move to the bottom of the window. On one knee, she knelt face to face with him. And like she had done so many times in her youth, she placed her lips to the window and let out a tremendous breath. With her pale finger, she countered his request. "I WILL CALL SOMEONE."

As she concluded her script, the young man smiled. Slowly he turned and trudged back to his car. The elderly woman, a bit surprised by her own actions, also smiled, if ever so slightly. She moved briskly away from the window to locate her telephone. The drapes, however, were left open.

That night, as she closed her eyes, she thought back to the day's occurrence. She had made a difference. Strange times. Strange times, indeed.

In a sense, the custom of teaching is the retelling of human existence. It is our unbridled parable that must include many voices in its chorus. As teachers, we look for innovative ways to allow the students' voices to be heard from every pinnacle on earth.

Mirroring the elderly lady in the previous anecdote, maintaining our stride is not an easy proposition. Life happens, and if we believe in a balanced existence, half of what we experience can be distressing. Yet, the impact found in our profession resides in our ability to affect lives, and our story is told in the enchanted relationships we build with our students, families, and each other. When we dare to connect, despite the risks, we foster the opportunity to be born again, and again, and again.

Hopefully, the charm of this text broadens the elderly woman's magical moment. We are a people business. We are of people. And the times shared among us are grounded in how we view and treat each other in relation to what we value. What is *hidden* resides in all of us. *It is our ability to discover the "relationship" in each situation that yields success for our lives.*

We all have our window, and at the right angle, it can present new perspectives while simultaneously offering a sincere reflection of ourselves, if ever so faint.

If and when we decide to mark upon it resides within.
Best Wishes.

Introduction

The Hidden Teacher looks to identify the various hidden messages that exist within schools by analyzing systems that revolve around human dynamics. The text is sectioned into themes, and chapters include concise vignettes, poignant discussions, and practical advice. In addition, each chapter includes real-world assistance for the classroom. Although each chapter can be explored in isolation, it would be beneficial to review each themed section in its entirety.

Part I examines ourselves in relation to our attitudes and aptitude for success. This section looks to establish one's passions as the focal point for extended positive success in and out of the classroom.

Part II is entitled *Classroom Dynamics*. In this section, student issues are explored to uncover bias and different ways to approach classroom management. Practical advice is provided for building successful protocols for attainable social norms.

Part III focuses on *Curriculum, Instruction, and Assessment*. Here, best practice strategies are identified to assist teachers in obtaining the most out of their lessons. Furthermore, scholarship is defined by its extension beyond the assessment with the hope of creating life-long learners.

Part IV revolves around culture. In this piece, the reader can explore how "we do what we do" in relation to language and comprehension. Reflective practice is suggested, as our ability to understand our patterns will assist us in unearthing sustainable relationships.

Part V focuses on *Relationships*. In being a people business, the more we can locate the "relationship" in each situation, the better chance there is to build a positive partnership. Identifying win-win situations is a mainstay of this section.

Part VI examines school systems. Here, the reader will discover configurations of winning for students—our ultimate goal. Understanding what the system is asking of us makes all the difference in our ability to be most effective.

Part VII is branded *Now and Zen*. Within these chapters, hope is presented as a precursor of all failure and success. Our ability to maintain a positive attitude, even when faced with trying circumstances, will ultimately support our ability to remain positive throughout our career.

Part VIII provides usable advice for many "common sense" situations that sometimes go unnoticed during busy times. The reader is provided a host of ideas to follow, while also bearing witness to situations/actions that should be avoided. Likewise, this section also provides the reader twenty case studies that can be used as anticipatory sets to the chapters or as extended discussion starters upon completion.

Part IX summarizes the premise that we must be aware of the various aspects of our profession that go unnoticed. By using both our brains and our hearts, we will have a more grounded view of success in relation to student achievement and ours as well.

I

Of Thy Self

JOURNEY JOYFULLY; FOR SUMMITS BRING END TO FOCUSED FEET.

ONE

What's in Your Cup?

Fred Robbins was a professional educator. A veteran teacher for over twenty-two years, Fred had seen his share. From lesson plans and state mandates to stress, strikes, and seminars, Fred had been there. This was not to say that Fred was a negative person. He definitely was not. Cautious, but not negative. And to the staff at Central Elementary School, Fred was affectionately known as Papa Bear.

As usual, Fred was selected to be a mentor to a new teacher. He loved the role and relished the opportunity to be part of a person's introduction to Central Elementary and, most times, to teaching. Part of the reason Fred enjoyed being a mentor had to do with his passion for teaching. He loved that feeling that you get when you know you have made the difference for someone. He embraced that sensation daily with his kids, but to be able to assist another adult was extra special. Plus, being a mentor excited him for the start of the year. That was until he mentored Rob Wise.

Rob Wise was a twenty-three-year-old rookie full of spit and vinegar. The type of guy you would have known in high school and thought, "He's going places." Rob was not mean-spirited. He was not malicious. Rob just knew things. Lots of things. And according to people who knew him best, Rob knew everything (or so he thought)! Needless to say, being a mentee was not necessarily on Rob's bucket list. But all in all, Rob was not a bad guy.

Pairing Fred with Rob was intentional. Dr. Shelly knew what she was doing. Her hope was that some of Fred's experience would rub off on Rob. Likewise, she had wished that some of Rob's energy would find its way to Fred. Unfortunately, the union was not a match made in paradise. Although Fred continually relayed information to Rob, he always felt that Rob was disinterested in what he was saying.

Although never a formal declaration, Fred granted Rob distance (the size of Texas). For Fred, it was about survival. "How many times can you bang your

*head against the wall before it starts to hurt?" Fred thought. "One's ability to
learn must be present."* In Fred's opinion, Rob's was not.

Fred did his best throughout the year to play along. He even delivered a
pleasant speech during the end-of-the-year new teacher ceremony. Unfortunately, Rob was not at the ceremony because he was coaching the middle school chess
team. True story.

There is judicious tale in Hobart's *Kishido: The Way of the Western Warrior*
that relates one of the greatest principles we can ever possess as a teacher—being accessible to new ideas. In the story, the student continually
interrupted the teacher as he tried to discuss the foundations to the discipline of Karate. As the student chattered, the teacher served tea. In filling
his pupil's cup, the master continued to pour the tea until the cup was
overflowing. The tea spilled everywhere. The student, now soggy, became disturbed and solicited a response from the elder. At that, the teacher explained that like the cup, the student's mind was too full and needed
to be emptied before they could begin their journey together. The soggy
student sipped and stewed.[1]

Both the story of the cup and Fred's interactions with Rob are connected. And on the surface, perhaps that old adage between youth and
experience plays a part. As the saying goes, "You don't get to be old by
being a fool." However, the constant struggle between these forces deserves a closer look when it comes to ourselves and teaching.

Why do so many sidestep the new opportunities as if these chances
were murky puddles about to mar our new penny loafers? As teachers,
we are the greatest pilferers in the world. Admittedly, we beg, borrow,
and steal from just about anyone when it comes to great ideas. Yet, our
insecurity in our own ability can sometimes hinder the process of collaboration, especially when we are new in a position.

As human beings, we want to be valued. We want to have purpose
and feel like we belong on our own merit (in addition to the fantastic
ideas we just borrowed at the last in-service day). This is not to attest that
everyone feels this way. Of course there are those who appreciate all of
the advice and guidance they receive. Such are the easy ones. If only the
task of teaching was that tranquil.

However, we make our bones with the ones who cannot be easily
reached. We find our triumphs in impacting the "spit and vinegar" kids.
Yet until now, perhaps the parallel between our behavior and theirs had
not been witnessed.

Think about the Robs you have encountered along the way. For what
were they searching? Respect? Acceptance? Here is where the deck flips.
Rob's fault resides in his cup. In wanting to establish himself as a con-
tender, he has mistaken wisdom for weakness. No one asked Rob to sit at
the kid's table during Thanksgiving dinner, and yet, his behavior would
suggest it occurred.

Teaching is a funny profession. We build our bread by being experts. And yet, so much of this job exists within the times we are not. It is almost like a broken buzzer on an alarm clock, striking at the designated time and continuing to ring deep into the day. The piercing jangle is like the babble from the so-called experts who look to establish their worth in their words. *But the truly wise understand the lips are the wrong starting place; it is with the ears that we begin to create trust and expertise.* As the saying goes, "Better to be thought the fool than to open your mouth and remove all doubt."

But this is an arduous proposition. As teachers, we like to talk. That's what we do. Again, the paradox to success presents full circle. The very best of teachers do less talking in their classrooms than their students. And this premise transcends the classroom to the hallways, the faculty rooms, the bus ramps, and so forth. Here is where Rob lost his way.

However, both Rob and Fred have a part in this failed production. Fred loved to teach; he loved being a mentor; but his mentoring methodology was linked to a traditional teaching style—teacher centered. Fred "relayed" information to Rob. His lessons were not interactive or discovery based.

Malcolm Knowles has dedicated a life's work at the study of andragogy, the learning habits of adults. He discusses the crux of self-directed learning, a kindred-spirit guide versus an omnipotent being. A copilot if you will. Suggesting, offering, but not insisting. [2]

This is not to say that the traditional, more directed approaches cannot be utilized. In times of crisis, be as directed as you need to be. However, a career is a long time. Every lesson of Fred's twenty-two-year stint does not need to be learned on day one, two, or 104! Time is on our side when it comes to knowing what is in our cup and what is in someone else's. A collaborative spirit is just that. It is a bond that joins people together in the name *and in cause.*

We know what is in our cup; we need to learn what is in others to be sincerely people centered. This does not diminish our authority but raises us above the need for rank without purpose. Mentors and teachers must focus upon building the bridge to the learner by involving him or her in the process and decisions of their learning. Team matters.

PRACTICAL ADVICE

Lead with your ears.

Silence is golden, especially when in new situations. This is not to say that one should not be involved. On the contrary, be passionate about what matters to you and jump in with both feet. Only listen first. Learn what others are thinking. Build off of their starts. And visualize the collaborative spirit that makes us human. Drafting is a powerful tactic in racing and in life alike.

Be the old dog learning new tricks.

The grizzled veterans of our profession do not have to be the stodgy naysayers. We all have a choice to make when it comes to change. Nothing is more inspiring than a master teacher modeling a fearless spirit when it comes to new ideas. Using tradition to limit progress turns folks off to the historical perspective and directs power toward the non-action.

FOR THE CLASSROOM

Instead of what you know; start with what the student may want to know.

One of the greatest tools we possess as teachers (as humans) is our ability to question. In your planning, build in the opportunities for your students to seek rather than to be given. Teachers who consider background knowledge and focus a keen eye toward student interest inspire even the most difficult of dispositions. Obviously, standards matter, along with the plethora of national and state testing. However, building an internal motivation (planning lessons with personal connections) makes even the driest of standardized assessment fun.

Do not give up on the Robs in your class.

The frustration that comes with a "know it all" has been documented. However, deep down, that person probably has some sort of insecurity tied to his or her personality. Although a scary proposition, try having an honest conversation with this person. Build the relationship by practicing a genuine desire to know his or her person. Remember, isolation wanes, but connections sustain. It is with the difficult that we garner an appreciation for what may be perceived as easy. Cherish the extremes and everything in between.

Isolation wanes, but connections sustain.

NOTES

1. Hobart, Peter. (2003). *Kishido: the way of the western warrior.* Prescott, AZ: Hohm Press.
2. Knowles, Malcolm. (1984). *Andragogy in action: Applying modern principles of adult learning.* San Francisco, CA: Jossey-Bass.

TWO

Put Your Passion into Action

What gets you going? You know, what are the activities that you love to do in life that really get your juices flowing? For some, traveling's the ticket. Be it a cruise to the Caribbean or a jaunt to Germany, experiencing other customs and cultures energizes some peoples' souls. For others, hobbies reign supreme. Maybe you are a musician or magician or maybe you enjoy skiing, diving, or just driving. Whatever your hobby, it is safe to say that when you are in the moment, there is no place that you would rather be.

Of course these activities do not diminish the passion we all have for our profession. To truly be a great teacher, one has to love it to the last. But it is interesting how some tend to keep their personal experiences and their teaching separate. Obviously, sharing a tender moment with a loved one may not be a solid topic for your next anticipatory set. We all understand the principle "friendly but not friends."

However, it is funny how those who keep their weekend lives so secret from their classrooms often are the ones who appear so unhappy. Tom was such a teacher . . . until a fellow colleague flung a friendly challenge his way.

Tom Brown knew he wanted to be a teacher his entire life. Both his mother and father were educators, and for Tom, it was only natural that he was going to be. Tom followed suit and became a high school math teacher. He adored the subject because math took the learner in so many directions.

Tom was a bear for detail and would often rehearse his lectures and lessons. Publicly, he said it made him feel more prepared for questions from the students. However, there was also an added benefit to the process. Tom loved to act. He loved to pretend he was a great mathematician discovering some new theory about fractions. Yet, he did not perform in class. None of his math mentors ever performed; who was he to start? It just seemed unprofessional for a math teacher to "entertain" in class.

Janice Jones was not born to teach; she was born to dance. A master performer, Janice had toured various cities and had even worked on Broadway. Now an eleventh grade English teacher, she was a catch to her class and colleagues. On numerous occasions, students entered class to music. Janice, still a gifted dancer, would twirl around the classroom handing out papers or whatever. The kids, at first, thought it was odd. But over time, they kind of respected the fact that this was Mrs. Jones, and dancing was her thing.

Tom did not dance, but always felt jealous of Janice's freedom. Routinely, Tom would steal a peek into her room as he strolled by during his prep period. As Janice would be doing the soft shoe as she stood at the board, he always wondered what was going on in her students' minds. Yet, he did not ask.

One day during lunch, Janice approached Tom near the coffeemaker. "You watch me from the hallway, but you never say a word. What are you thinking about Thomas Brown?"

Tom was taken back. He politely smiled and tried to dismiss the attention with a simple, "Oh nothing," but Janice would have none of that. She followed him to the table. She sat across from him and smiled. "Well," she said.

Tom went on to explain how he admired her guts to dance in front of her students. In being "more reserved," Tom could not see himself being able to generate the nerve to be that open. Janice continued to press him.

"The students tell me you are a whiz at numbers, but a bit dry with your delivery. Ever think about doing something different?" She challenged in a playful manner.

"What do you mean?" He asked. But Janice did not reply. She just smiled and drifted out of the room.

Tom sat for a while. It was his moment, and he had been called out. He finally ascended with a grin on his face. He knew what he had to do and wondered if Mr. Venter, the play director, had a cloak that could fit him for tomorrow's discussion on integers.

Too often, we suppress our "what ifs" with "what's been." Tom, in staying with tradition, did not see the potential of unleashing his inner being. Luckily, Janice's playful manner and simplistic challenge hit a nerve. Did she know he liked to act? No. But she knew he liked *something.* The key was breathing life into the idea.

As teachers, that is what we do. We employ our subject and standards. But the real thrill occurs by inspiring someone to try. We become more creditable to our students to follow their dreams when we live the motto as well. Janice was a testament to this belief. Each stride told the students it was okay to be yourself, to dream big and be happy being different. That is what fearless passion gives us—a chance to truly live.

The Toms of the world are not bad people. They just are. And they reside in both adults and students. Teachers that sustain in a positive manner find a way to bring their passions into the classroom while also offering students a chance to find theirs. The exploration into the enchantment of our souls sustains the happiness we so desperately need to maintain positive, productive careers.

Remember, passion drives our existence. Although we assumed teaching to be our focus, each of us possesses a burning desire aside from the daily duties. Our ability to bring our passions into our teaching is the critical connection in sustaining a successful attitude. Likewise, our skill in assisting students to locate their passions by developing instruction that garners this practice will vitalize both their growth and our own.

PRACTICAL ADVICE

If teaching is your second profession, go do your first.

Those who have selected teaching as their "back up" profession tend to be the most bitter in the building. Reward requires risk. If you were the type of person who did not take a risk, but now holds a grudge in the classroom each day for those who did, please do us all a favor and find another job. The "would be" professional singer turned music teacher tends to silence a ton of voices during the course of his or her tenure.

Do not allow your passion to overstep the work.

Just because you are a gifted bassist does not mean that playing the bass everyday will work for your science class. Balance is key! Our first responsibility is to our students and the job we are hired to perform. That's the salad; our passions are the dressings that add flavor and variety. Remember your primary function.

FOR THE CLASSROOM

Keep it professional.

Although it goes without saying, let's say it anyway. You may be a dynamic comedian, but it does not mean that your act will hold up to tenth grade students. Stay grounded. Remember, your professional nature builds respect. Performing a soft shoe in class is one thing; the tango is quite another.

Help the students find their passions.

Plan for exploration and expression. Solicit ideas from the kids. Build in flexibility for explanations. The more you can create an atmosphere of safety, the more students will be willing to take risks in front of you and their peers. It cannot be just about us.

II

Classroom Dynamics

THEY DON'T CALL IT ROCK AND ROCK!

THREE

"What to Do with Johnny?"

Assume you are the assistant principal in this building and analyze the following situation:

Mrs. Sanders, a good-hearted teacher, has a problem. Johnny Wiseman was late to her homeroom again. In fact, this is the third time this week he has been late. Mrs. Sanders has written a referral and is asking you to discipline him because "if we allow Johnny to be late, what kind of message are we sending to the other students?"

Mr. Bell, the school guidance counselor, has overheard this conversation. After, he feels compelled to inform you that Johnny's father walked out on the family last month. In fact, he believes that since Johnny's mother has to work two jobs now, Johnny has had to make sure that his sisters get on the bus to attend elementary school, a possible reason for his morning lateness. In overhearing about the referral for Johnny, he implores you not to discipline him.

When you check his attendance record from the previous year, you do notice that Johnny, although not a discipline problem, has been late before (prior to his father's departure). In fact, one could make an argument that he has a lateness problem.

Knowing that the discipline policy calls for a two-day internal suspension and a citation for truancy, which could be a $100.00 fine, what will you do with Johnny? Be sure to address all possible stakeholders in your response.

School and Society by Feinberg and Soltis, is an excellent resource when thinking about relationships in schools. Within the pages of this text, the authors identify the connection between school and society by capturing the essence of how schools operate and how folks respond to the system. [1]

Feinberg and Soltis speak of three explanations—*functionalism* (school functions to teach us how to live in society—focusing on the rights of the collective), *conflict theory* (school serves to keep the majority in power—focusing on the rights of the individual), and *interpretivism* (school depends—focusing on the argument at hand and not a global philosophy like functionalist or conflict theorists).

For the benefit of our conversation, let us think of these theories as human beings. A functional person sees the world as black or white. And you guessed it: Mrs. Sanders represents a functional approach. To her, allowing Johnny to "slide" would cause a problem, not necessarily with Johnny, but with the other students. But is this the right way to act on the part of a teacher?

In our schools, teachers can often take the form of functionalists. Their jobs ask them to service students *many to one*. In other words, most teachers look to the needs of the group with relation to the needs of the individuals within the group. Stands to reason.

Teachers deal with many students at one time and are sometimes forced into a "fair is equal" approach just because of sheer numbers. It is not unlikely for a teacher to explain that "If I do that for you, Johnny, I would need to do that for everyone else." Not necessarily the answer Johnny was looking for, but one that he can somewhat understand. Teachers are charged with establishing norms they can achieve for the entire class.

Although some of my colleagues would scoff at the latter explanation and state that teachers need to "go above and beyond for each child," we cannot diminish the system's expectations on a teacher. It is not easy servicing fifteen, to twenty to thirty students per class per period, when a third or more may have IEPs.

On the other hand, guidance counselors, special education teachers, school psychologists, and so forth play a different role in the system. These folks view the system from the needs of the *one-to-many* (conflict theorists). Their day-to-day tasks place them in a position of defender, whereby the individual elicits the attention. The one child's needs trump that of the masses or the necessity to have consistency among them. When writing an IEP, classroom implications do not precede individual expectations. It is all about this child, the one-to-many mantra!

In our case study, Mr. Bell is our conflict theorist. His concerns in this situation focus on Johnny (the one) in relation to an already unfair situation (his homelife). Mr. Bell would see the need to break the rules for Johnny because his circumstance do not fit the prescribed pattern.

Both the functional and conflict theory approaches bring with them bias about the system. Their philosophies hinge on believing prior to the actual action occurring. In other words, a functionalist, aside from this situation, looks to build equity in the name of being fair. Conversely, a conflict theorist does not see systems as fair because their structure hinders those not in charge. Therefore, a conflict theorist would always see the system as a hindrance to equity.

Finally, an interpretivist does not see the system as a positive or negative. It just is. Interpretivist opinions and actions are grounded on what needs to happen based upon the local needs of the situation. In other words, fair depends.

In this situation, you were placed in the position of being the interpretivist. This is not to say that every administrator is one; however, the system is designed for them to make the call within this instance. Often they are asked to balance the rights of the individuals and the rights of the collect. In a sense, they are asked to "interpret" situations as they reside between the two philosophies.

How does this research fit into our conversation, especially for teachers? One of the greatest factors that influence our system sometimes goes without ever being mentioned in the conversation. That factor is the system and the dynamic components to the people it serves. *Examine* people's place within the system and sometimes we can learn more about ourselves and the pressures that are placed on us to secure the needs of all. (In other words, what we might view as personal may not be.)

The key point in any decision between the individual and the collective is to eliminate bias. To do this, we must arrive at each action as a stand-alone and not part of a past philosophy that is guiding our thinking. For example, what if you asked a child to read aloud in class, and she refused? Would that be okay? Suppose she was recovering from laryngitis? Would that change your opinion? Would it be all right for the next child to refuse without having an illness? Now add this exchange to topics like lateness, bullying, and so forth. Does being guilty ten times make us guilty the eleventh prior to the investigation?

In eliminating bias, we must not pass judgment based upon prior action or a belief system that would assume innocence or guilt prior to the action. If we took a functional point of view, the student in this case is guilty—a where there is smoke, there's fire. Within a conflict theorist model, the system is ablaze and the individual is used to getting burned.

The smart move is to take an interpretivist stance, whereby we waive a decision until we have investigated thoroughly. By determining the most logical sequence of events (the circumstances that define the action), we can move to judgment without the pangs of conscience that arrive when we assume truth without knowledge.

Being a teacher is one of the most demanding, most dynamic jobs in the system. And although the needs of the collective drive our global planning, our most penetrable inroads are made when we break through the system's pressure to see what is needed for everyone. Fair depends.

PRACTICAL ADVICE

See the philosophies at work.

Once familiar with these ideals, you will see them like a Megalodon shark swimming in a stream. The sooner you grasp the patterns in your thinking and that of your colleagues, the better prepared for situations and conflict you will be. Likewise, the opportunities to perform the research prior to judgment will serve you well both in and out of school. Equal is equal; but fair depends.

Share what you know.

Establishing a vernacular builds understanding and trust. Whenever possible, talk about these philosophies and their impact on people. Challenge others (nicely) to negate their bias by stating it prior to judging. Building a consistency for consistency's sake does not necessarily lead to wins. Sure, it is a cleaner approach, more favorable to control freaks, but that is not reality when dealing with human beings.

FOR THE CLASSROOM

Apply this thinking to your classroom management structure.

In teaching these concepts to the students, you will be able to set the tone to make judgments based upon what is best for the child and not what is expected by the masses. By exposing the students to this thinking, you will also build trust with them that you are not just making a whimsical decision or playing favorites. *Everyone attains what they need.*

Consider the system when dealing with parents.

The next time someone asks you to be part of a 504 meeting or to work on an IEP, understand that the parents' philosophy will be grounded in *one-to-many*. In other words, using defense tactics that place the rights of the collective over the individual (their child) will just upset the situation. Try to see what the need is and tactfully try to explain your points if the recommendations are unreasonable. Remember, they already think the system is broken, hence the reason they are attending an IEP or 504 meeting. Make it a more amicable scene for all by seeing the starting points of all the players.

NOTE

1. Fienberg, W., & Soltis, J. F. (1998). *School and society.* New York: Teachers College Press.

FOUR

My Miracle

Of all the goals you have achieved, of every summit you have climbed and conquered, what do you think is your greatest accomplishment? Some in our profession would point to earning lofty degrees; others might share a story about a struggling student whom we were able to reach. Whatever the event, these milestones serve as a reminder of why we wanted to be in education and motivate us for our next pinnacle.

In being reflective, how do you think our parents would answer the same question?

In dealing with a disruptive student, a teacher friend of mine, Donna, once had a parent teach her a very valuable lesson:

Donna was a sixth grade technology education teacher. In being a specials teacher (not core content), Donna's schedule spread across the grade levels, and her class sizes were relatively large. Donna was very adept at handling student issues, as warranted by her being named Teacher of the Year three times in the past decade. However, on this particular day, Donna was a bit distracted.

Unfortunately, her purse was missing, her classroom supplies were moved from her room, and her grades were due today at 10:00 a.m. Needless to say, it had been a busy morning—not to mention, this was day three, period two—her largest class.

At the end of a very exhausting period, Judy, a very quiet student, approached Donna to solicit some assistance in finding her missing book bag. Donna, almost fried at this point, directed her to look through the storage rooms again. Donna went about her business and never gave the situation a second thought until Judy's mother called her the next day.

During the conversation, Mrs. Moore, Judy's mother, expressed her displeasure with the way that Donna handled her daughter's concern. Mrs. Moore felt like Donna neglected to really assist her daughter. In fact, her daughter said she felt as though Donna had "better things" to do.

In not trying to be defensive, Donna attempted to gain empathy, clarifying what a crazy day it had been. Mrs. Moore understood, and for the most part, was okay with her reasoning. Yet, Mrs. Moore ended by explaining to Donna that Judy was "her miracle." And that she would hope in the future Donna would see her, and every child, as one so not to put a thing in front of a child.

At that moment, Donna knew she would never forget this valued experience.

When we are involved with school situations, sometimes it is easy for us to forget that the child in front of us is someone's miracle. On that fateful day, Donna was tired and a bit put off, and can honestly admit her mind was on other things. Mrs. Moore could sense Donna's frustration and assumed that her demeanor was a reflection on her child and not on the goings-on of her day.

There is an enormous difference between getting something done and getting it done well.

In this instance, Donna had neglected to demonstrate her compassion and understanding that would come with working with someone's miracle. By placing the issues of the day in front of her student's needs, she unfortunately gave Judy a false impression.

When dealing with our families, it is critical to see things from the parent's perspective, especially when it comes to bad news (discipline, grades, etc.). Think about it—the parent is home or at work. They have a host of issues they are dealing with on their own, and then we call them with our news.

It is natural from them to be startled and get defensive—they are hearing about how "their miracle" did something wrong or performed poorly on an assessment. Sometimes, they look upon this event as a reflection on their parenting. Other times, a parent might recollect to their days in school and transpose their experiences (positive or negative) onto the current situation.

When dealing with families, we must remember that each child is someone's miracle. This does not excuse behaviors, but only looks to serve as a barometer on how we are approaching the situation. This type of passionate methodology is often the center of various student resolution models, but it can also serve as guide for all interactions.

PRACTICAL ADVICE

Stay calm.

People are going to be upset with you in this job. It is just going to happen, no matter how compassionate you are. Do not take it personally. Stay in control and allow the person to talk it out. Do not raise your voice, for that never bodes well when your boss learns of it (even if the person deserved it). Plus, you want to show your colleagues/students that you are always in control, no matter how hot the issues get. Stay calm. Listen. Talk slowly.

Adults are miracles too.

Interestingly, just as the children are our parents' miracles, the staff also has family that holds them in lofty regard. When dealing with issues that could cause people to get upset, set the stage for compassion by recalling the initial premise. Follow the golden rule. Present yourself with compassion and dignity. Always be the professional.

FOR THE CLASSROOM

Judge the action, not the person.

In our position, there will be times when we have to judge the actions of students; however, we are not asked to judge them as human beings. Even in the worst situations, stick to the facts and allow an unbiased process to commence. Maintaining an impartial stance serves the greater good beyond the incident. Everyone makes mistakes; do not make the next one by condemning a child based upon a "one and done" mentality.

Always be professional in the classroom.

Remember that Dry Idea deodorant commercial slogan, "Never let them see you sweat"? Well, this tag could be a motto for a successful classroom management strategy. When we lose our cool, students lose faith in our ability to bring a sense of safety to their learning environment. By staying in control, we establish trust and let all the students realize that no matter what the situation, we will handle it with dignity and respect.

FIVE

Counter Melodies

Rita Walls, a high school chemistry teacher, was serving on the district's strate-
gic planning committee. Excited to be part of the process, she eagerly attended
each session, determined to make a difference. However, during the course of
these gatherings, it had become apparent that her view of running the perfect
meeting was certainly not the way of the presenters. And this discrepancy was
starting to annoy her.

Rita was a planner. She was an organized individual and certainly did not
leave her lessons to chance. She was a chemist. There was a methodology to her
craft. In finding faith with order, she was having a problem with the laissez-faire
approach of the presenters.

Of course she believed that each individual had the right to be heard. Any
scientist worth her salt would appreciate the need to analyze possible outcomes.
What was driving Rita batty was the dialogue. It was incessant. People went on
and on, and just when the group thought it had consensus, someone would make
a comment that would cause the group to reconsider its position. Why was it so
difficult to make a decision? Why did the presenters allow the meandering babble
to continue?

Meeting after meeting, Rita became more frustrated. "These people are mad."
Finally, she stopped attending the sessions altogether. Wasting time just would
not do, especially for busy folks.

Two months later, the plan was completed and implemented with the staff.

On the surface, who can blame Rita? We have all been at meetings where
the only consensus is no consensus. At these summits, frustrations can
run high, and spirits can clash when disagreement presents with no end.

However, if it is possible to have two differing approaches that can
yield similar results, then the realization of success or failure as it relates
to our actions is a bit more complex with regard to our values (linked to

expectations, motivations, etc.). In other words, regardless of Rita's opinion, the meetings did yield an outcome.

Music is a magical part of so much of our lives. It has the potential to move us physically, intellectually, emotionally, socially, and spiritually. Music truly encompasses the human spirit.

One of the most recognizable songs ever written was the theme song by John Williams from *Indiana Jones.*[1] (Are you humming it right now?) One of the reasons it is so recognizable has to do with its catchy tag. That distinctness of the trumpet's march gives it such an adventurous flair that the song almost defines the premise of exploration even without the pictures.

Yet, what truly makes this song move is not necessarily the blast from the brass but the drive of the drums, accompanied by the surrounding instruments. (When you get a chance, take a moment and listen to the song again. Try to direct your ears away from the main melody to the rhythm. Here is where the adventure begins.)

As with music, life has a rhythm section. Sometimes, it is in direct accord with our thinking, and sometimes it is not. Yet, the counter melody often supplies the friction for movement. Sadly, many tend to only want to hear *their* melody.

Sometimes, our emotions can hinder us when it comes to the idea of embracing the antithesis. Too often, we view these options as untenable because they serve to place us in a position of uneasiness. In the educational profession, people make their mark by knowing. However, what might be more beneficial is to understand that human beings, and the manners in which we get things done, vary. In this instance, knowing the options may be just as valuable as knowing a single answer.

Rita was a scientist. She was used to proper procedure and practice. Unfortunately, human beings do not always act in correct fashion, and there is more than one way to secure the end result.

Negotiation leads to cultural change. It requires us to reconcile with the possibility of not getting our way. When we agree that what we most believe to be false is possible, we allow ourselves the strength of the option. Hence, we do not back ourselves into a corner, but allow flexibility to formulate all opportunities. (Yes, despite the chatter, it is possible for a perceived unproductive meeting to have benefits—the counter melody at work.)

Language is power. The ability to communicate on so many levels of understanding is priceless. Yet, there are two words that generate the thought process like no others. Those two words are "what if." What if this meeting is different? What if we used professional development days to write curriculum? What if advanced placement classes were double blocked? What if? What if? What if?

In music, sometimes the counter melody provides the driving force for the main tune to shine. Our ability to not only expect the antithesis of what we believe, but to start with it might be the single greatest lesson learned when dealing with human beings and the glorious deviation that comes with difference.

PRACTICAL ADVICE

Embrace the gray.

If you are the type of person that only sees the black and white in situations, you may have some long days ahead. When dealing with human beings and formal culture, there are going to be many times when the "correct" answers do not exist, thus forcing us to live within the gray.

For instance, just because the discipline book states a person receives a two day suspension for being insubordinate does not answer the question, "What does insubordination look like?" Our understanding of social situations and appropriate actions/non-actions will guide numerous conversations in a constant search for what is right for your school. See it all!

State your case.

Too often, we tend to suffer in silence instead of voicing our feelings for fear of reprisal. In a courteous manner, Rita could have approached the speakers with suggestions. Maybe there were others in the room who felt the same way. Obviously, we do not want to embarrass anyone, but showing concern about the process is a good reason to spark a necessary conversation. Just be nice about it.

FOR THE CLASSROOM

Use the opposite to spur thinking.

One of the greatest lessons I had ever witnessed was in a math class where the teacher asked the class to disprove that two plus two equals four. Talk about great brainstorming. Too often, when we are trying to introduce an idea, we do our best to prove our point first to secure favor. However, perhaps starting with the antithesis is a better plan. If the teacher establishes correct, creative thinking yields to lower levels of knowledge by recalling someone else's logic.

Use alternative assessment structures and choice.

Learners digest information in different fashions. In accordance with this theory, the presentation of mastery must also be fluid. Allow your students choice and flexibility (where possible) to prove to you that they have attained the concept. The journey to the summit yields wondrous gifts along the way. The more paths that are being taken, the more chances students will have for discovery. Start with divergent questions; plan for the dialogue, not the answers.

NOTE

1. Williams, John. (1981). *Indiana Jones: The Soundtracks Collection.* Columbia Records.

III

Curriculum, Instruction, and Assessment

NOT ONLY WHAT, BUT WHAT IF AND WHY!

SIX

The Buoyance Trial

Carol, a well-respected teacher, was about to teach buoyancy to her 7th grade class in a suburban school. Knowing that this was always a problematic topic for her students to comprehend, she thought about best practice and decided to connect with the topic with prior knowledge and student interest—making the learning engaging and a "real-world" experience. Residing only a short distance from the New Jersey shoreline, she decided to utilize the idea of surfing and connect it to the Water Games (as seen on TV). In fact, she designed an assignment for her class to actually make one and had a contest ready to go for the boards that would float.

The miniproject would be started in school (design, directions), and students would have to utilize a few items from their homes. Really excited about trying something new and linked to a solid methodology, she proceeded with her plan. (Do you think this is a quality lesson for the standard of buoyancy? Will students enjoy it? Would you?)

Truth be told, Carol proceeded with her plan, and of her five science classes, almost everyone succeeded in securing an amazing grade. Almost everyone . . . . Unfortunately for Carol, almost everyone was not good enough. She chatted about the lesson with her fiancé, an accountant. Being a "numbers guy," she was used to his deductions.

When she was finished explaining the assignment, the process, and the outcome, Charles glanced and grinned. He then asked her a question that not only changed the preparation for this lesson, but transformed her entire teaching philosophy forever. His question was, "Do black people surf?"

As one ponders this question, please realize that the shock value was planned. Likewise, note that the term *black* can be substituted for any specific group of people who do not mirror the majority.

In this particular situation, the school resided in a predominantly white neighborhood. There was a basic standard for economic stability between the races; however, one could note differences in culture. And in this case, the black people were not regular viewers of the *Water Games* and certainly did not venture to the New Jersey shoreline at the number that the white folks did.

Now be honest. Did you think this was a pretty good lesson when asked in paragraph one? If you did, you are not alone. At first glance, this assignment appears rock solid. Active participation, hands-on learning, and real-world connections are mainstays of best practice methodology. To be able to teach to the standards is essential, but to actually design the interaction and exploration for the learner tells the tale of legends.

Carol did think about culture, in that she wanted to connect the learning to familiar entities. Yet, her inability to think beyond what was normal for her (and the majority of folks) caused the divide. She unfortunately was not thinking about multiple perspectives. In other words, her inability to establish a preceding protocol for her teaching allowed for innocent indifference toward the non-majority (not intentional, just unaware).

By no means does this chapter serve as the only manner in which to address the cultural divide. There are a host of other texts, such as *Understanding Multicultural Education: Equity for All Students* by Christine Rogers Stanton and Francisco Alfonso Rios or *Race, Ethnicity, and Socioeconomic Status: A Theoretical Analysis of Their Interrelationship* by Charles Vert Willie, that do an outstanding job defining the concealed flaws in schools, systemic racism, and a host of other relevant topics to the issue of cultural and teaching.[1]

The worth of "The Buoyancy Trial" has to do with our ability to take a complex topic, such as culturally competent teaching, and break it down to usable parts for classroom success. For if we cut through the research, *what speaks to us as human beings is our innate desire to be known.* This connection to self and others germinates the seeds of self-esteem, motivation, and ultimately achievement. For too long, waves of good-hearted educators have planned tremendous lessons without establishing the root for those successes—knowing the students, seeing color, and fine-tuning our craft.

Consider the following account for context:

Each summer, Henry's family (Caucasian) would vacation (you guessed it) at the Jersey shore. When asked, Henry remembered the excitement that accompanied these jaunts to the beach and wanted to share these experiences with his friends, especially Lynne, an African American woman.

For years, Henry had been asking Lynne to bring her family to the beach with his. He would constantly badger her about how much fun it would be to have their children play together in the sand and surf. Ironically, the more he asked, the more she politely dismissed the premise. Curious, he continued to nudge her.

One day, Henry called her from the boardwalk to harass her about enjoying some caramel popcorn together. With what must have been a marvelous amount of nerve, Lynne asked him to count the black people on the boardwalk.

Henry stumbled over his words and asked her to repeat the command. She said, "I want you to count the number of black people who are on the boardwalk right now and do not include anyone who is working."

Henry glanced around and started to count. The boardwalk was pretty white. "The number is three," he said softly Knowing that there were about two thousand people in his sightline was humbling.

Lynne went on to explain that she did not mean to embarrass him. She was not blaming him for enjoying the beach. She just wanted him to see what was not there. Until that moment, Henry just didn't notice. Such are the unobserved nuisances of classroom dynamics and achievement for all.

Henry and Lynne talked for hours after that about race, culture, and a bunch of other things that he never thought he would with another person who did not look like him. But he was lucky, he had Lynne, and she was willing to take him there.

It is incumbent upon us, as educators, to become Lynnes in our thinking and planning. We must engage in the process of seeing what the naked eye does not—going where the path does not readily go. And these illuminations do not have to just be about race.

In a faculty in-service, I once heard a teacher state that he wished students could overcome the habit of labeling "different as weird." Admittedly, this simple statement holds great truth within. Brain research will tell us that our minds want to make connections. Schemas want to associate, almost like a computer that wants to label and save documents in tidy folders. The fault occurs when we make these associations based upon difference to the norm rather than individual worth. And sometimes, our virtuous nature misses the signals to these phenomena.

Scores of texts have been published about the topic of achievement gaps; yet, often times when the book ends or the presenter leaves, it becomes too easy to revert to what we "live" as normal. What is needed is a daily reminder, a mental tickler if you will, that brings us back to center when it comes to issues of race and culture in schools.

Perhaps the simple motto "*Know me* " could serve as a precursor to planning. "Know me" asks the user to consider the individual traits of each child to establish a connection to him/her through not only our instructional practices, but also ourselves. This adage reminds us that until we make that connection, until we cement this ideal in the forefront of our minds, we may miss opportunities to reach all students. "Know me."

PRACTICAL ADVICE

Find your Lynne.

Although easier said than done, how can we educate students we do not know if we do not secure trust in our journey? Obviously, we do not want to take the advice of one person to speak for an entire group of people, but building our cultural conversations breeds confidence in addressing the next one. Establishing a trusted colleague can be the greatest life experience one can have. In the meantime, read, read, read. Building a knowledge base will assist us in this critical mission.

See color.

How many times are people asked about race only to state that they "do not see color in their classroom?" It is time we took this perceived politically correct terminology out of our vernacular. See color! Appreciate its brilliance and genuinely seek to know more about things we do not. Ask questions; be an active learner. Taking an interest in someone is at the heart of cultural competent teaching. One cannot mandate a moral imperative; but realizing and verbalizing the differences serve to spur action.

FOR THE CLASSROOM

Use the data.

One of the best places to start in terms of impacting your classroom is the data. Look at your standardized achievement scores. Review your teacher assessments. Break it down. What trends do you see? Think about the instructional practice you invoked. Did it provide for choice and input? Sometimes, the best way to plan with others in mind is to engage them in a dialogue. Ask and you shall receive.

Live the motto.

When planning a lesson, think about maxims like "Know me" or "It's about this child." Let them be reminders that every face in your room needs to read stories where the protagonist looks like him/her. Also, forge this line of thinking in your noninstructional preparation. Bulletin boards, book selections, and various other tools must encompass a community feel.

Likewise, there is no magical formula for achievement for all students. Connectedness spreads the seeds of lifelong learning. Break through the fear of the unknown by making your classroom a place for all students. See color.

NOTE

1. Rios, Francisco A., & Stanton, Christine Rogers. (2011). *Understanding multicultural education: Equity for all students*. Lanham, MD: Rowman and Littlefield Education. Willie, C. V. (1983). *Race, ethnicity and socioeconomic status: A theoretical analysis of their interrelationship*. Lanham, MD: Rowman and Littlefield.

SEVEN

Critical Connections — Start with the Why!

Lonnie and Tambi Williams are both educators and dear friends. On many occasions, we have pondered various educational topics stemming from policy and practice to structure and systems. Often the debate is spirited, as all of us love a good conversation. However, when it comes to considering best-practice instruction, Lonnie has an amazing personal story that summarizes one of the most critical lessons teachers can evoke in the classroom:

My wife Tambi and I are blessed with having three daughters, and to this day, they are our greatest treasure. Although they are each uniquely different and special in their own way, there is a certain characteristic that the two older possess (and we are sure that the baby will too) that connect them as a family. Be it dinner, bath, or bedtime, Tambi and I can be assured that somewhere in our conversation, one if not both will question, "Why."

Although tempted, we do our best not to answer their questions with, "Because we are your parents." This is not to judge anyone who utilizes this tactic, and truthfully, from time to time, it is necessary to take a more direct approach. However, our decision to take the time to explain the thinking behind our decisions allows our children the opportunity to increase their curiosity and thirst for understanding. Now, this may sound all well and good, but in times when we are in a hurry to get to grandma's house, those repeated "whys" can honestly be trying.

Sometimes it takes an enormous effort to constantly explain ourselves when the decision has already been made. However, we hold to the belief that children who question tend to be children who succeed, and thus, do our very best to accommodate their inquiries.

As one can imagine, the initial "why" is followed by another, and another and another. And as the trip goes, so too does our conversation with our girls.

These dialogues often expand beyond the initial question to include a host of other situations that exist beyond the literal. What started with, "Why do we have to go to grandma's house?" evolves into questions like, "Why does grandma live there?" and "Why do we call her grandma?" These discussions represent one of the thrills of being a parent—witnessing our girls gain resilience and confidence in their learning. Is it tiring? Absolutely! But we would not want it any other way.

Again, both Lonnie and Tambi are wonderful people, and their words motivate positive action. When children ask "why," they are making an attempt to broaden their understanding of the world by connecting what they know with a rationale for what they do not yet understand. In doing so, they challenge their brain (and ours) to think beyond the literal action of taking a trip to explore the significance of the trip with relation to themselves and their world. ("Why do we call her grandma?")

"Why" forces us to explore our thinking to produce viable justifications. If a child asked, "Why do we have to go to grandma's house?" and parents responded with, "Because we are your parents," we may have established ourselves as an authority (which can be a confident gesture), but we have effectively cut off what could be have been a valuable conversation. (Again, there are instances when a more firm response may be necessary; however, to solely define our decisions as edicts compromises our ability to allow others to make connections.)

In considering this anecdote, one can start to take into account the message with relation to the purpose of our educational system. Our responsibility, as educators, is to inspire our students to want to attain their personal best. One of the greatest skills we can develop is the ability to inspire thoughtful questioning techniques in our students. These purposeful inquiries produce higher-order thinking, thus creating new connections to their world.

Without establishing said connections, we are bound to exist on a technical level, which does not answer questions of why we learn what we learn other than for the technical end of proficiency attainment. This idea is best demonstrated in the answer to the following question. Have you ever had a student ask:

"WHY DO I NEED TO KNOW THIS?"

If the answer is "because it is on the test," we have reverted to the technical level and thus eliminated the process of establishing another level of culture, a deeper meaning to extend our learning to include real-world connections. In a sense, *we have informed our students that once the test is over, it is okay to forget about the lesson.* Be it math, science, music, or art, we must link the learning in each class with an overarching ideal that is connected to the real world.

Much of the inspiration behind this chapter comes from the principle that each learning experience is both unique and related at the same time. For example, learning about recycling in science class has value when it comes to the act of recycling or the processes needed to accomplish the actual task. However, aside from the scientific composition of materials or system for accomplishing the actual recycling, there exists a host of possible connections that teachers outside of science could make such as moral imperatives, laws, cost values, and so forth. Learning a skill is valuable (unique), but being able to unite that skill to our world provides a more robust learning experience since it requires us to access higher-order thinking to accomplish it.

One of our most critical undertakings as educators is to assist young learners to make connections to their individual worlds to develop the capacity for higher-order thinking that is relevant and useful. By establishing the process of connectedness, we can begin to explore the commonalities that exist beyond our specific genres to access both the literal and thematic meanings, thus, accessing *our* thinking to assist theirs.

Being a father has made all the difference in Lonnie's life. Although we were all young once, to be able to witness another person being curious and passionate about their learning has been truly inspiring for him. It is that sense of wonder that makes being an educator worth the sweat.

By establishing a thematic rationale for learning (beyond the standards), we can again rediscover the thrill of learning to connect teacher to teacher, teacher to student, student to student, and student to the world.

PRACTICAL ADVICE

People over products.

Whether in the classroom, hallway, or faculty room, remember we are in a people business. Behind our litany of actions reside the reasons for them. Get to know people on a genuine level. Go beyond the typical weather and weekend chats. Take a sincere interest, listen well, and remember for the next occasion. Nothing makes more of an impression than to recall a lone detail about someone weeks later. Locate the whys in their life.

Recall chapter 2.

Just as you have passions, so too do your colleagues and students. Take a sincere interest in what excites them. Ask them probing questions, look at pictures, and make connections. Suggest that they bring their passions into their classrooms and help their students to do the same. The legs feed the wolf, but our passions feed our heart. Establish the why beyond the classroom.

FOR THE CLASSROOM

Use motivation theory.

Build your understanding of sustainable student motivation by funneling your lessons through intrinsic values. By utilizing this approach, you will establish the connection to the personal learner, thus giving reason to sustaining the knowledge after the assessment has come and gone.

Give your lessons themes.

Just as stories contain both literal and metaphoric meanings, our subjects can too. We need to make the effort to connect our curriculums to expand thinking for both ourselves and ultimately our students. Survey

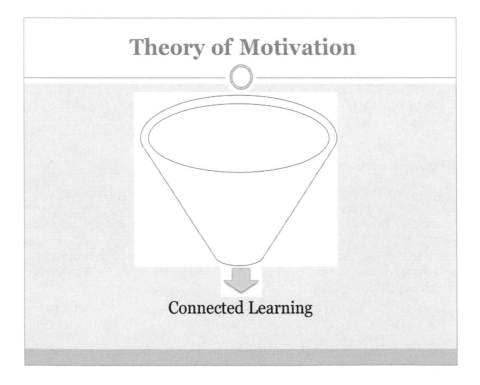

Figure 7.1.

your students. What are their interests, hopes, and dreams? How can you take your subject and connect it? Better yet, can you solicit their connections and be flexible enough to allow it to happen for each individual learner? Here is where the master teacher resides.

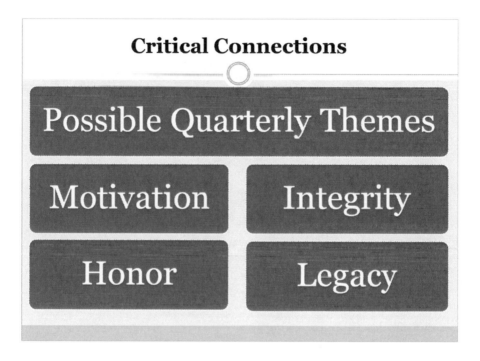

Figure 7.2.

EIGHT

"Behind the Curtain" Is the Gold!

Were you disappointed when Dorothy discovered that the Wizard of Oz was just a man operating the great machine from behind the curtain? I know I was. How could they travel all that way, take on all those scoundrels, and thwart the wicked witch just to discover the wizard was a fake? Serious questions for youngsters and adults to consider.[1]

Now, if you have not seen the *Wizard of Oz*, that's okay. The journey to Oz happens daily when someone decides to follow a dream and goes through great lengths to attain it. Teaching is like the journey to Oz. There are no promises at the end of the "yellow brick road." And yet, we press on.

As the journey from teacher-centered teaching gave way to student-centered teaching, it would be foolish to think this transformation is over. Like Dorothy, our search for the "wizard" in teaching persists. But what if the desired destination was located in the unveiling of the tricks behind the curtain? What if the evolution of teaching practice demanded the need for educators to open the deck and reveal all of our concealed strategies? What if?

Best practice needs to be circular in its inception, delivery, and resolution. We, as teachers, through our experience with best-practice concepts such as anticipatory sets or closing activities, have various tools in our toolbox to utilize when designing instruction. Students do not . . . until now!

Have you ever observed a teacher with great command over instructional practice? Chances are she has worked at her craft away from the eyes of the masses. Fluid movements do not occur accidentally. And yet, what if her practice involved the students in learning the very strategies that were intended to be used with them? Furthermore, what if the students were asked to analyze said strategies with another student? *In a sense, maybe the highest level learning occurs when students are engaged in trying, failing, and ultimately understanding the practices (behind the curtain) of teaching combined with the strategies and subject material.*

There are thousands of classrooms utilizing a similar style, and this discourse is not meant to imply that we have discovered the "Oz" of teaching. Yet, sometimes creating a vernacular for learning supports our level of understanding. *Student-centered teaching is good; but* student-taught learning *is crucial in creating learners who understand and can contribute to the process.*

Authentic student-taught learning generates opportunities for students to focus on others and their learning. In creating learning opportunities for others, students not only have to demonstrate a mastery of what they know about a given topic, but must also apply higher-order thinking strategies to be able to engage others in the process of learning. Please do not be mistaken by the simplicity of the charge. Students are not just creating instances of learning for others (games, power points, etc.); student perspective is being shifted from the products (a paper, presentation, etc.) to the process (creating a problem for another utilizing the content, strategies, and teaching practice).

For example, if a math teacher wants to give her students word problems to solve and teach to her class, we would attain a deeper understanding of not only the original word problem, but also the task analysis behind what goes into understanding a word problem by asking the students to think about possible ways to teach it. Once they have explored the options, they could select different variations in creating new learning for other students—a far cry from the days of chalk talk at the blackboard.

Why change? Why now? There are a host of factors that are contributing to the need. From the explosion of information, to the constant battle between which standards should be utilized for which test, educators are at a crossroads. In addition, one of the rationales for this type of shift in teaching practice stems from the concept of *the "selfish" learner*. To understand its premise, consider this situation for contextual perspective:

Many enjoy the ritual of giving, yet the basic premise behind the concept could create a paradox for those who truly enjoy being generous. For example, if a parent loves to give to her child because it makes her feel good, the adverse impact may be to create a child who is the antithesis of the parent's intentions. The parent did not aim to create a spoiled child; however, by not curbing the "desire" to give, she could have unintentionally positioned a detrimental value system upon the child. ("No more candy before dinner!")

However, there is a way to be generous and not create the unintended consequences. If a parent enjoys being generous, she needs to involve the child in giving to various others. In this fashion, the parent and child are both giving . . . the parent is giving the child an opportunity to give; *the child perhaps is doing*

Curriculum Mapping

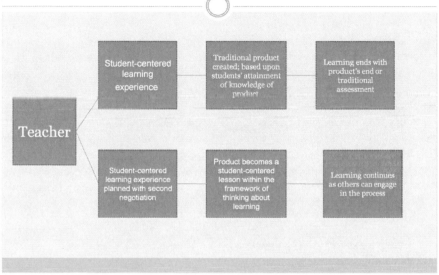

Figure 8.1.

the physical giving. Obviously, this pattern can take various forms. The take-home point resides in recognizing the pattern and addressing it as soon as possible. ("Let's take some of that candy to the shelter.")

Perhaps this very pattern plays out in our schools. We, as educators, want to give the best possible instruction to our students. Throughout the years, we have learned that the very best instructional practices are student centered—giving the power and choice to the student. Yet, in this intentional giving, are we creating learners who are selfish within the framework of expectation of power? In other words, much like the plight of our parents, if students only receive, and have no opportunity to give, the expectation may naturally be to always want. Call it an intellectual greed or just a lack of caring about the next learner or experience of learning.

If a teacher is designing a student-centered lesson, for it to be truly beneficial to the whole child, the lesson must end with a second negation of power between the student and another entity. (The first negotiation takes places between the teacher and the student—teacher gives student choice, privilege, etc.) For example, if an English teacher is designing a lesson around persuasion, and the student can demonstrate her mastery of this concept through a myriad of choices (an essay, speech, role play, etc.), the presentation must offer an opportunity for the student to "give" power to others. One such way could be attained not by giving them the answers (writing the essay, giving the speech, *etc.), but perhaps by posing the problem in a format that calls for a greater understanding of how we learn (student as planner, thinker, facilitator, and teacher).*

The connection to the premise comes to light when we consider that most of what we ask students to do ends with a product. But truly revolutionary learning is like an impeccable game of tag. We need to redesign our lesson plans to include the planning and best-practice teaching strategies.

It is up to us to create the capacity for our students to think beyond the product, to become interactive with the concept and the process, and to allow the phase of "lifelong learners" to start within the very premise of what we believe best practice to be. Just as Dorothy was able to make it home despite the circumstances, we too can create the means to the ends of student achievement.

Teach the students what you know about teaching along with your standards. Show them the magic and ask them to share the tactics with others. Teach them to fish. . .

PRACTICE ADVICE

Embrace why.

Be it in the classroom, at home, or wherever, appreciating the themes in life offers us a glimpse of a person's motivation. Those who view opposition as a threat choke the desire to grow in others and ourselves. Plan for the antithesis. Expect and embrace it as if an old friend from college was visiting. The mightiest of brains knows that their cup has more to hold.

Likewise, extending one's practice by taking classes or seminars only adds to our ability to gather more information, confidence, and ultimately, the ability to witness more possibilities.

Relationships breathe.

Teaching people to fish who did not know they were hungry can be challenging. Yet the consequence of not doing so builds a layer of dependence that is hard pressed to be broken. Within your relationships, understand there will be times to speak, times to listen, time. Equipping others with strategies to analyze their social situations is like teaching students how to teach. Both the learner and the teacher benefit from adhering to a mantra of "we must strive to understand what makes us unique."

FOR THE CLASSROOM

It does not have to be done every day.

The teaching profession sometimes resembles an all-or-nothing paradigm. New ideas do not have to be implemented to exactness from now until Mars. Understood, this style of teaching takes multiple layers of preparation, and there will be days when you simply cannot do it. That's okay. As you begin this journey, you will be amazed when you are in the middle of a "typical" lesson and a student calls out, "You just asked us a divergent question." On those days, smile. Know that the thinking beyond the topic is occurring on multiple levels.

Avoid the technical.

It is understood that a reading specialist may not be able to demonstrate all of what he knows to a child with the hopes that the child will be able to "do" what he does. However, just by sharing in the conversation of "why" the child is being asked to do something, is the start for understanding that each utilized practice has an intended outcome. If a student can verbalize what a strategy is supposed to do, and can analyze if it has occurred or not, the learning shifts from even the most passive exercise to one of activity involvement. Now, have the student share the pattern with another student in the form of a question, and the interactive lesson becomes a reality.

NOTE

1. Baum, Frank. (1900). *The wonderful Wizard of Oz.* Chicago, IL: George M. Hill Company.

NINE

Prove It!

Coach Browning was a woman of conviction. Having been a member of a state championship volleyball team and now coaching and teaching at her alma mater, anything less than 100 percent just would not do. In fact, some would say Coach Browning was the most determined member of the East High School staff.

Coach was not mean, but motivating. Her unbridled passion for the sport of volleyball was only surpassed but her desire for her students and players to succeed in life. She genuinely treasured her job and looked forward to each day. In fact, she would always say that she "never worked a day in her life" because she absolutely loved what she was doing.

Coach Browning was a motivator. She loved to razz her players when she thought they were selling themselves short. She did this by utilizing simple, yet very poignant proverbs. One of her most prolific statements was "Opinions are like arm pits; everyone has them, and they all stink" (not necessarily the type of simile one can use in the classroom, but on the court, it worked). Unnecessary to mention, a player hearing these words from Coach's mouth understood it was time to step up and prove she belonged.

We all have probably met a Coach Browning in our travels. Sometimes, coaches get a bad rap for not being academic. However, when we gaze further into their methodology, we can find a host of best practice techniques being utilized (even if they appear to be wily witticisms at first).

With this example, Coach Browning has articulated one of the single greatest factors to student achievement—being able to prove one's position. Although not communicated in an "academic manner," Coach Browning understood the nature of inquiry, the process of investigation and discovery. For her, the conception of truth started with an assumption that what is real must be verified. In other words, without some sort of substantial evidence, truth was left to interpretation.

For example, when teaching a match point serve, Coach Browning would ask each girl to practice it over and over and over again. In never knowing who would be the person to take that serve with the game on the line, everyone had to be ready. It was not good enough to just practice it, but all players were required to receive not only a thumbs up from their coach but from their peers as well. This demonstrated verification and also built the concept of team.

Whether in an academic setting or on the playing field, students are asked to define not only what they know, but how they know it. In fact, this premise is one of the glue points that unite all subjects, only we rarely think to see the connections. For example, consider the following question:

IF YOU COULD ONLY TEACH ONE PROCESS WITHIN YOUR SUBJECT, WHAT WOULD IT BE AND WHY?

We all have a plethora of different topics and standards that must be accomplished by year's end; however, if you were limited to just one process, just a single progression necessary for the child to attain some level of success in your classroom, what would it be?

For math teachers, maybe it is the art of solving equations (showing your work of course). For science, the scientific method might be at the top of the list. Social studies might look at the legal process of establishing the argument; perhaps language arts might select persuasive writing or thematic interpretations. Hopefully, the association comes to focus.

Common language plays a huge part in this discussion. Schools sometimes forget to point out the connectedness of language when it comes to instructional practice. For example, what may be the scientific methodology in one class could resemble the problem-solving matrix in another. As teachers, we must look for the ever-present bond that exists in the depths of best practice—the power of affirming one's learning.

All of these processes find their fidelity in asking the learner to "construct" an argument. In simple terms, take a position and "show me" you know what you know with evidence. However, despite their seemingly obvious correlation, we sometimes fail to establish that union with our students.

As teachers, one of our prime responsibilities is to establish a motivational level beyond the classroom assessment. Within this premise, the need to acquire lifelong skills is apparent. It is with such skills that the reciprocal nature of "lifelong" extends from classroom to living room.

This connection to home also establishes the wherewithal for intrinsic motivation as well: "When learning is driven by students' own questions and connects to their own understanding of the world, motivation is natural and intrinsic. Through this approach what students learn in school helps them to understand what they experience outside of school. And their outside experience is called upon to help them make sense of what they are learning in school."[1]

For too long, this type of instructional practice has been limited to the gifted and talented classroom. Here, one can find the highest levels of Bloom's Taxonomy and Webb's Depths of Knowledge being attained through self-selected means. Classrooms are built by student interest, and motivation is sustained by the delivery of ownership. Sometimes this is not the case in regular classrooms.

The latter statement is not accusatory. Being a teacher is one of the most challenging occupations going. But perhaps the subject and standards limit our perception of what is possible. Here is where those darn state assessments can lead us to the abyss of skill and drill.

One of the major underlying themes to discovery is the thought process that accompanies the journey. And to assist our students with making the learning more than just an "armpit," we must design lessons that require evidence. Notably, we must work on our students' "grit factor" by planning meaning-learning experiences, grounded in personal connectives. We must check our assignments for assistive reflection and help them stay focused on what is fact and what is not.

If we are able to do this, we will establish the affirmation necessary to sustain one positive learning experience to the next one, and the next one, and . . . .

PRACTICAL ADVICE

Build common language.

Try to simplify the process of proving one's point by creating common language. Simple sayings like "Prove it" or "Show me" force the learner to demonstrate mastery through a process of persuasion and discovery. If one of the ultimate educational endeavors is the dissertation, it seems to make sense that ministudies should be occurring throughout one's educational journey.

Do your homework.

Have you ever tried to debate a topic with someone who has no technical experience? Chances are, those discussions become more about containing emotion than serving as a means to possible consensus. Those who argue from a state of emotion lack the practical expertise to make a sound, rationale one. Be sure to do the research prior to passing judgment. Gossip has no proof; opinions have no pity.

FOR THE CLASSROOM

Be sure the process ends with evidence.

If you could only ask students to answer one question after the assignment, perhaps it should be, "How do you know what you know?" Establish a basis for the argument by creating instruction and assessments that necessitate more than just one's opinion. If a learner can conquer this dimension, she will certainly be able to wander merrily during times when no proof is necessary. If one can make a three-point turn, the assumption that a one-point turn is possible is a pretty sure article.

Provide choice where you can.

Internal motivation rises when personal needs are met. Remember the gifted education model of accelerated extension. If you can allow your students the freedom to select the journey, you increase the desire and grit factor. Plan for their plan.

NOTE

1. Kuhlthau, C., Maniotes, L., & Caspari, A. (2007). *Guided inquiry: Learning in the 21st century.* Westport, CT: Libraries Unlimited.

IV

Culture

*DOING THE RIGHT THING IS EASY; DECIDING ON WHAT IS RIGHT
IS HOW THE HUMAN EXPERIENCE ENDURES.*

TEN

The Conversation Upstairs

Consider this conversation between two PE teachers in a typical school:

BUD: (cheerful) Good morning, Phil. How was your weekend?

PHIL: Okay, I guess. Nothing special. Yours?

BUD: Good. Had the grandkids over to the house. Louise and I love it when they visit . . . and when they go home. (Both laugh.)

PHIL: Yes. I can imagine. Janice and I are in the thick of it now. The twins are running us ragged.

BUD: That's what they are supposed to do.

PHIL: Well, I would definitely give them an A for their effort. If it is okay with you, I'd like to use the outside courts first today. I have my crowded class.

BUD: Not a problem.

On the surface, this conversation is as innocent as the drifting snow. Two colleagues having a Monday morning chat before they kick off their PE classes at Anytown High School. As one could imagine, this exchange could be occurring with varying topics in literally thousands of schools across the country and beyond. Such is the art of connection.

However, what if we add a bit of articulation to the dialogue? How would a few add-ons change this original exchange?

BUD: (Matter of fact) *Good morning, Phil. How was your weekend?*

PHIL: *Okay, I guess. Nothing special. Yours?*

BUD: Good. (Rolling his eyes.) *Had the grandkids over the house. Louise and I love* (said with emphasis) *it when they visit . . . and when they go home.*

PHIL: *Yes. I can imagine. Janice and I are in the thick of it now. The twins are running us ragged.*

BUD: *That's what they are supposed to do.*

PHIL: *Well, I would definitely give them an A for their effort. If it is okay with you, I'd like to use the outside courts first today. I have my crowded* (said with emphasis) *class.*

BUD: (shaking his head in disgust) *Not a problem.*

And so the conversation upstairs commences. We all understand that what we say sometimes plays second fiddle to the way we say it. And this short account hopefully demonstrates the change in demeanor that occurs. The power of our nonverbal communication extends from the literal to the abstract and can make a potentially innocent conversation loaded with advanced meaning.

Consider this—What if there were no idle conversations? What if every utterance from our lips reflected a deeper meaning beyond the literal words? In other words, although we hear a person's precise words, perchance there is another conversation existing beyond the syllables and substance. Seem far-fetched?

It should not be that foreign to believe that we "use" language to communicate meaning. In a sense, we foster ideas in our brains and look for manners to communicate these ideas in overt and covert ways. For example, have you ever witnessed someone flirting with another person? Funny how the discussion about someone's summer vacation can have nothing to do with the sand and surf and everything to do with "I hope he thinks I am interesting" or "Maybe she'll think I am cute." (Remember Rudolph?)

Whatever the means (the vacation talk), the conversation that is playing out above the words stems from the hidden message of how human beings converse. And it happens in an instant!

Our brains are amazing. To think how incredible the design is; to be able to have multiple levels of communication (verbal, nonverbal, overt, covert, etc.) simultaneously is remarkable. Reflective questions such as, "Why am I saying what I am saying? Why did I select these words?

Could I be more direct without being offensive?" zoom by us like rockets in orbit, awaiting the final destination—the purpose of the interchange.

If the latter premise has merit, then this idea of being the dynamic communicator in the classroom brings with it consideration. *We use language to establish ideas, but the ideas can sometimes be lost in the translation depending on which level of conversation the listener comprehends.*

For example, take our flirting fellow. What if his boss wanted to "see him in her office"? Does that statement mean that she is romantically interested in him? Chances are that if he arrived at her office in a smoking jacket with two glasses of bubbly she might have an issue with it. And yet, she just might be interested in him. Such are the dynamic possibilities when we combine meaning and language. (Please do not show up in your boss's office in a mood and blame this text. You are on your own for that one.)

It is incumbent upon us, the educators, to be aware that different levels of meaning exist when it comes to communication. We need to be mindful of our words, but perhaps more so of what message is being received by the listener/observer. Both the language and the intent as to why we are using the particular words matter.

How does this notion relate to the profession of teaching? When a child says, "I hate this class!" perhaps the verbatim meaning suits his intent (he really, really dislikes the class), but on many occasions, the initial wordage carries with it a host of other meanings. Many of our students want to be heard, but cannot present in a candid manner. *Be it the cultures of the classroom or the building, relationships are built upon communicating and the subtle and not so subtle interpretation of the meaning.* Therefore, it is inherent on the teacher to politely probe when in doubt. Arriving at the essence of an issue builds consistent connections.

PRACTICAL ADVICE

Be cautious about what you are "saying" without saying it.

Being cognizant of the nonverbal nuances in our communication patterns will help us to develop trusting relationships. There is nothing worse than leaving a conversation trying to figure out what message was being relayed. The more comfortable we are with folks, the more direct we can be, thus limiting the need to interpret what we initially cannot perceive. Build trusting relationships by speaking truth and verifying the message.

When in doubt, ask clarifying questions.

One of the greatest tools a person can use in an interview is to ask if all questions have been answered thoroughly. Do not limit this skill to just interviews. Too often, we leave conversations open to interpretation. If you wish to create a vague statement, then so be it. If not, be sure to solicit feedback and offer clarification where necessary.

FOR THE CLASSROOM

Limit sarcasm.

Nothing is more damaging to a teacher-student relationship than the imbalance of power that sarcasm delivers—especially with "innocent" jokes. If there is a target (a person) for a comment, refrain from using it. Furthermore, be as passionate with student-to-student relationships as well. Make the classroom a bully-free zone in actions, words, and intent.

Utilize proactive and reflective practice in conversations with students.

As educators, there are numerous times we second guess a lesson's worth or a particular piece of a unit plan. Keep this tactic in the foreground as you consider conversations. Likewise, some of the most skilled speakers in the world practice their words and mannerisms to ensure consistency and approach. Within the framework of planning your next lesson, think about what and how you are going to communicate the message.

If it seems reasonable to assess the acquisition of standards, it must also resonate to test comprehension of critical conversations. Make sure you know.

ELEVEN

"All I Do for This Place!"

Regan Troy was a third grade teacher with an expertise in literacy. She was an excellent educator and was involved in a myriad of school-sponsored activities. In fact, she was a woman on the move! From the science fair and math counts club to the holiday teas and lunch bunch treats, Regan was a backbone for many of these wonderful events.

Although the parents, students, and even the principal praised her efforts with these activities, her colleagues were a bit wary to hand out the cheers. Never formal, some of her comments during the crunch times of these events were concerning.

Nonetheless, Regan continued to volunteer and the months turned into years. Five to be exact. At which time, Mrs. Deeds, the principal, had decided to make a few grade level changes to the staff. Seems there was an influx of students registering in grade one, and Mrs. Deeds felt it best to place a few more experienced teachers in that grade to balance the teams. Sound reasoning, but when dealing with grade changes, "sound" presents to people's ears in different tones.

Lo and behold, Regan was one of those being asked to relocate. Understanding it would be a tough moment for folks, Mrs. Deeds met with each person individually. Some were happy; others were disappointed. But most understood the move and accepted the reasoning. Most, except Regan.

Unfortunately, Regan lost her composure. While meeting with Mrs. Deeds, she sat like a statue, awaiting her turn to respond. Mrs. Deeds could see that she was visibly upset.

"Are you okay?" she asked.

At that, Regan burst with a litany of events and activities she had been involved in over the years. When questioned why she was listing these items, Regan replied with "I would think that a person that has given so much of herself for others would not be treated with such disrespect."

Mrs. Deeds went on to explain the decision and the rationale behind it. It was not personal: she needed Regan. However, Regan's tensed lips and curt nods were telling. Meeting over.

Once back in her classroom, a few of her colleagues came to see her. Without soliciting, Regan stated, "All I do for this place and this is the thanks I get. Well, she can find a new sponsor for all of those things. I'm done!"

Regan had spoken the truth, for next year she taught first grade and did not volunteer for a single event. Although never said to her face, several of Regan's colleagues remarked how well the activities ran despite her absence.

Stay in this business long enough and most certainly there will come a time when you feel duped. This is not to say that there was some malicious plan behind your demise within a given situation, yet in times of distress, there are those who believe the gods were against them from the start. In this circumstance, Regan embodies an unfortunate misconception when it comes to the act of doing and the expected recognition that follows.

For schools to function to the degree they do, all of us are asked to assist with the extra. Whether a paid position or strictly voluntary, the events that surround the lessons are like rainbow sprinkles on tempting ice cream sundaes. They accent the structure of the system. However, our purpose for partaking in extracurricular activities can be as endless as one's selection of flavors. (Make mine a butter pecan with chocolate sprinkles, please.)

Look, we all do for some sense of personal gain. We do. It is okay for us to see the benefit for ourselves and others when we participate in such work. Yet, the folks who gravitate toward the kudos instead of the work often end up negative and angry.

Perhaps Regan's response started five years prior. Maybe she really did not have the time to offer, but felt compelled to volunteer because she was new or thought that her principal would look down upon her. The trouble with this situation stems from the lack of conversation about her circumstance. It is okay if you cannot give the time because of other commitments. We just need to communicate it to those involved.

For example, Brody, a friend of mine, is really uncomfortable in public settings. Although a gifted speaker, he is by nature an introvert. And needless to say, big parties or social events give him a massive amount of acid in his belly.

Despite the GERD, when asked by his girlfriend to attend these events with her, he reluctantly attends and spends the next four hours miserable, making his girlfriend miserable having to explain to her friends why Brody is so miserable. Know anyone like this?

Perhaps an honest conversation could assist both Brody and his girlfriend. Go for half of the time. Pick one event a month. Don't leave her side. Whatever the compromise, the discussion is warranted. The hushed appeasing only leads to an eventual confrontation—plus a heck of a lot of coin on antacids.

And yet, there are those who are just egomaniacs, desiring everyone to look at them. These people feel that doing one thing garners favor for future paybacks. Nonsense! These people should be assisted in their thinking or avoided, for their intentions and actions cause negativity to abound.

Statements like "All I do for this place" breed a false sense of ownership. We lease; we rent; however, there is no option to buy. If you are feeling taken advantage of by someone, talk about it. To lead with "pedestal" statements only brings distance between you and your colleagues. Do because you want to do, not because someone is watching. If the plaudits from the masses come, so be it. And if not, that's okay. Create opportunities for service. Remember, character is who we are, not what we do.

PRACTICAL ADVICE

Celebrate others first.

If God's hand intended the mouth to be more important than the ears, he would have given us two of those instead of one. Find worth in service. Do because it is right for you. Do because it connects with your passion, makes you feel whole, and helps others. Yes, it is okay to want to coach because you need the money, but place the benefit of your actions for others over personal gain. Heck, just put them in balance and that would be a great start.

The show will go on.

If for some reason you were unable to make it to your classroom this year, the principal would not pack up your room. Someone would be there. Lessons would be taught and students would learn. We all must appreciate what we have while we have it. Again, being a teacher is not a life sentence; it is an opportunity. Embrace it each day.

In addition, do not be upset if you read this chapter and thought, "This is me." One of the greatest parts of life is our ability to transform. It is never too late to begin anew. Find your center; surround yourself with positive people and have at it!

FOR THE CLASSROOM

Build assignments/assessments that force thought beyond the grade.

One of the greatest tragedies of our profession is that some fail to connect their content beyond an assignment or assessment. Students need to understand how this knowledge impacts their lives beyond the test. Even with standardized assessments, look for ways to present information that is connected to their (age appropriate) real-world setting. Although obvious, this concept sometimes gets lost in crunch time. Questions like, "How can you use this information at home?" generate authentic learning.

Praise all publicly; praise individuals privately.

External motivation only goes so far in sustaining achievement and consistent effort. In other words, students that hitch their horses to the success of others often get stuck in the mud. Sustained motivation comes from within. When handing out the kudos, consider this premise in your classroom. In addition, look for opportunities to secure learning. Build character through generous and selfless acts.

TWELVE

"It Is What It Is"

As teachers, much of what we do revolves around being in control. This is not to say that control in and of itself is negative, only a realization that being organized is paramount in our profession. In knowing that much of our day is spent planning outcomes, it is no wonder so many teachers find comfort in establishing the known. Pearl Farley was such a person.

Venture into Primer Elementary School on any given weekday, and you will be able to find third grade teacher Pearl Farley alone at the copy machine. Part of the reason why she is alone has to do with the time. It's 5 a.m. The other part has to do with her attitude. You see, Pearl dislikes distraction.

Pearl is a creature of habit, and she's been "doing it this way" since well before some of the staff members of Primer were born. She realizes that things happen (copier jams, coffee spills, etc.), and therefore, assumes not much will be happening at 5 a.m.—a small price to pay to stay on target with the day's plans.

Pearl is not an aggressive force at Primer. She just is. In being so matter of fact, her unadorned demeanor can be interpreted as negative, especially when she uses one of her famous clichés when faced with issues that go beyond her control.

As teachers know, things change. There are a myriad of people (administration, politicians, other teachers, etc.) who, by the nature of their job, impact the classroom. Although their influence is not always negative, some find any impact on the classroom to be stressful, especially Pearl.

Be it a new vocabulary program or a math supplemental series, Pearl's standard, "It is what it is" can be felt from the lunchroom to the classrooms. And this submission to the inevitable helps to create a feeling of helplessness, especially for the new folks who feed off of this veteran's mentality.

How many times have you heard "It is what it is?" Seriously, I would bet that at least seven to nine times a week we all come in contact with someone who uses this cliché. And most times, they are not presenting it in a positive manner.

Clichés present double meanings. First, the literal meaning represents an obvious known. In other words, it *IS* what it is. (Reminds me of that professional football coach Dennis Green who, when referring to an opponent at a press conference stated, "They are who we thought they were." Very funny.) Such an apparent acknowledgment almost represents a repetition of the current situation.

For example, if someone came up to you and said, "The car has been stolen," and you repeated, "It is what it is," it is almost like saying, "The car has been stolen." In simple terms, the literal usage of the cliché serves as a replication of fact.

The thematic significance commences when we interpret the message. When someone states, "The car has been stolen" and another answers with, "It is what it is," this response creates a feeling of helplessness. In other words, we realize the car has been stolen, and there is nothing we can do about that situation. Bummer!

The encroachment on teachers' domain has been steady; and, the assumption that folks are under the microscope these days is apparent to say the least. With state assessments and new teacher evaluation systems, it is no wonder teachers are feeling a loss of control. Safe to say, it has become difficult to continually adjust to others' interpretations of what is right for one's class. When folks become despondent about situations that limit our ability to plan for outcomes, we, as teachers, get distraught (and rightfully so).

Think about this. When you were dreaming of becoming a teacher, did you say to yourself, "Gosh, I cannot wait to compromise. Gee, I cannot wait to yield to someone else's way of thinking. Yippee, I get to share my classroom." Needless to say, many of us did not wish in these terms.

Obviously, compromising and sharing are critically important, and one would never want to downplay the significance, but when most dreamed about teaching, those dreams were usually of the individual and the students. (I imagined the energy of the classroom to be like a magic carpet ride, taking us to new and interesting places. What a trip!)

As teachers, we enjoy the challenge of achievement for all. And we realize when the door closes, it is up to us to deliver on the mission. Sometimes we look at those trying to "change" the classroom as people who are hindering our ability to succeed. Yet, to survive this system, we must realize that we cannot control everything, and we certainly are not alone in our planning and purpose of student achievement. So what can we do?

Of course we can get up at 5 a.m. and get to the copy machine before everyone else and hope that the person before did not leave it with a jam; however, if that schedule does not work for you, perhaps taking the power back in your thinking will. Variations in our intellectual processes are not absolutes. We cannot look at every instance of change as permanent oppression on our plans.

Clichés that dominate void conversations. Too often, we utilize a cliché when the imbalance of power tips away from our favor. "It is what it is" is one such platitude that reflects a powerless feeling. Perhaps adding two words to this cliché could make all the difference—not only in our attitude, but also in building conversations that can lead to positive change: "It is what it is—*for now.*"

"For now" builds faith that although a situation may appear to be hopeless, both time and impact can create a new change, thus assisting us with the original event. For example, suppose while eating your favorite pistachios, you crack a tooth. You could say, "It is what it is," and wallow in pain and despair. Or you could think, "It is what it is for now," pick up the phone and call the dentist. We may not be able to control the outcomes of every event, but we can control our thinking. Staying positive is key! Recognize the clichés in your repertoire, then work hard to substitute true dialogue for them.

PRACTICAL ADVICE

The hallway is the dentist.

It is funny how during the most critical points in our lives (birth, surgery, traveling by airplane, etc.) we are asked to give up control. What makes this such a paradox is that we are rewarded daily for being in control. To survive the system, we must see the gray in our world. For example, folks that look to control every nuisance in their classroom really struggle when they enter the hallway (life outside our domain). We must look upon the hallway like going to the dentist. We can commit to having our tooth fixed (the positive), but then we must surrender the control of the outcome to the expertise of another.

Organization creates peace of mind.

Again, there is nothing wrong with planning. If getting to the copy machine at 5 a.m. eases your anxiety concerning getting it all done, then so be it. Look for ways to build in proactive approaches to your daily routines. And if someone does leave the copy machine jammed for you, take a deep breath and know that it will be okay.

FOR THE CLASSROOM

Organization creates peace of mind for your students.

Obviously, the students have less control over the planning of course content and such, but those teachers who have excellent organizational skills help students lessen their anxiety. Just as a teacher will sometimes state, "Tell me what you want me to do," so too do students think in terms of task accomplishment. School is difficult enough without having to trudge about with a disorganized teacher. Plan with purpose.

Teach this concept to your students.

Being able to process your feelings is a sure way to extend your enthusiasm for life. We all have stress, and change can be difficult. Being able to articulate your emotional state to a colleague or friend assists you in living the human experience. Remember, clichés stop conversation when most needed. However, if you cannot live without the platitude, be sure to at least add "for now" to its end.

V

Relationships

ASSUME GOOD INTENTIONS UNTIL PROVEN OTHERWISE;
THEN FORGIVE.

THIRTEEN

The Conspiracy Theorist

Francine Meyers was an excellent assistant principal, and when the principal of Eugene Elementary School took a job in another district, the entire staff was hoping Francine would get the nod.

Eugene Elementary had its share of vagabond leadership. In fact, this was the third principal to vacate the position in the last seven years. Francine had been an assistant to two of them, and in being a former Eugene teacher, dean, and now assistant principal, she was the natural pick of the staff. She knew the teachers, the families, and the students. And her presence in the school was a breath of reassurance and consistency amid the early exits of the former principals.

As the hiring process commenced, Phyllis Murphy, a lead teacher at Eugene, was pulling for Francine to get the job. Yet, despite her vote of confidence, she warned the staff not to get too excited because "you know how those central office folks can be." In fact, Phyllis insisted that if Francine did not get the job, central office must have it out for their school. Although not outwardly, teachers did harvest some ill will toward central office for their choice of principals who certainly did not work out over the last seven years.

Lo and behold, the day of the announcement came, and the superintendent visited Eugene. During the faculty meeting, she announced that the committee decided to hire Dr. Brooks, an elementary principal from another district. Needless to say, you could hear a pin drop. The blank stares from the teachers told the story. Phyllis Murphy shook her head in disgust as she whispered to her table, "I knew they were going to do this. They don't care about what we want. I heard Dr. Brooks worked with the superintendent in another district. What favoritism! Poor Francine."

As the meeting broke, several people came up to Francine to give their condolences; however, Francine stayed professional and assured them that things would be fine.

67

Why does reality TV sell so well? Perhaps it has to do with our innate desire to feel safe. In other words, sometimes watching others live their lives in a public forum safeguards us from the harms that may befall the participants.

The same sense sometimes comes upon us while driving. For instance, you are in your car and hear the sudden siren of an ambulance. As you pull over to the side of the road, the first thought obviously goes to the health of the person in need. Yet, the next one sometimes goes to ourselves and our families to feel thankful the ambulance is not for us. This is not to say that we are malicious folks. Certainly not. But the feeling of security is reaffirmed when we witness someone else in a tangle that we do not have to face right at the moment.

Having power over our situation also brings a level of comfort and status. When we witness a competitor getting voted off an island or losing the big sing-off, our status can sometimes build in the face of our colleagues when we utilize the standard, "I knew that was going to happen" or "I told you so." Such is the motive of the conspiracy theorist and her desire to gather prestige and power.

Phyllis Murphy is our conspiracy theorist in this example. Her actions and words are guided to the heart of securing a "functioning" rationale to explain actions that cannot be readily defined. But why? Perhaps Phyllis's guiding philosophy has much to do with why she does what she does.

Recall chapter 3 and Feinberg and Soltis' lessons about functionalist, conflict theorist, and interpretivist.[1] Remember, a functional person sees the world as black or white. Fair is equal to this person because the system (the situation) is set up to reward equity (everyone the same way). Conversely, a conflict theorist believes fair is not equal because the system is already slanted against the individual. In simple terms, a conflict theorist believes the system is set up to keep the leaders in power, thus thwarting the efforts of the general population.

Finally, an interpretivist understands that fair depends upon the situation, the facts, and so forth. An interpretivist does not rush to judgment prior to understanding what is needed for the situation to be rectified.

In our example, Phyllis would represent a conflict-theorist approach because her thoughts point to a system (and the people controlling it) that is corrupt. For example, when Phyllis insisted to folks that if Francine did not get the job, central office must "have it out for their school," she set the stage for an "us versus them" situation. Once Dr. Brooks was named principal, Phyllis's prior proclamation grew wings; however, what facts were in place to solidify this stance to be true? You guessed it—none.

Conspiracy theorists believe what they believe prior to any action taking place. They "know" the outcome prior to the facts of the case because they judge the conditions instead of judging the actions. For instance, Phyllis "knew" that Francine was not going to be promoted not because of Francine's job performance (or any other facts surrounding her value to the organization), but based upon central office, which was already flawed prior to needing a principal. Figure 13.1 presents this scenario.

Even though we realize no substantial investigation has occurred, what Phyllis has produced is a false logic that loosely connects to a series of events that may or may not be in direct correlation to the premise of central office being corrupt.

Yet, what is flawed in this situation may be Phyllis's logic. Do we really believe central office wanted the three previous principals to leave? In other words, do we truly think central office "has it out" for a school? Are they not connected to the success and failures of the school as well? What inherent benefits might come from those folks having ill will toward Eugene? (We do realize that the antithesis provides benefits that one may not be able to perceive, but for this example, to believe that the central office purposefully picked three principals because they knew they would leave seems remote.)

The conspiracy theorist searches for patterns; once located, those threads are connected to aid the so-called "hunches" of the conspirator. Sure, there are those who are able to dismiss Phyllis's whims as nonsense; but sadly, many bystanders fail to thwart her conclusions and start to build a subconscious connection to the original thought. In other words, "Maybe central does not like us. Maybe Francine did something wrong?"

Step 1	Step 2	Step 3	Step 4	Step 5	Step 6
Pre-Conditioned Philosophy	An Action Occurs	Judgment Made	No Investigation	Philosophy Combined With Action To Create Conspiracy	Value is Established
Phyllis believes central office is flawed.	The position of principal opens.	"I know what will happen."	No evidence is gathered	Phyllis "knows" Francine will not get it because central office is "out to get them."	Outcome is perceived as negative.

Figure 13.1.

Furthermore, a person who leads with either a functional approach or a conflict-theory approach always ties personal outcome to any situation. For example, Phyllis and her cronies see Francine's dilemma as negative. Yet, an interpretivist's view allows the option of observing events as neutral because sometimes the outcomes do not impact us (see figure 13.2). However, when we lead with a hunch, the outcome has to have some sort of value to us (either we were correct or not correct).

In schools (and in life), we must see the damage the conspiracy theorist creates to the individual's and the organization's overall health. By fabricating bias, the conspiracy theorist manipulates time, injures reputations, and sabotages the culture of the building, all while securing power and prestige for herself. Although human beings find security in knowing, there will be times when we do not have the answers. The urge to assign value to an event without the facts must be prohibited.

Those who spout false prophecy do it as a precursor to the investigation. In other words, teachers who "know what happened" prior to knowing the facts cause great harm to the system by substituting their personal bias for a methodology for analyzing the facts.

As it turns out, the superintendent of the school had a prior conversation with Francine about taking the position as the middle school principal (hence why she did not seem that upset when Dr. Brooks received the nod). Within the year, Francine took the job and is doing wonderfully well there. Phyllis, however, also saw that move as a snub to Eugene. Go figure.

Step 1	Step 2	Step 3	Step 4	Step 5	Step 6
No Pre-Conditioned Philosophy	An Action Occurs	Judgment Made	Investigation	Philosophy *Is Not* Combined With Action To Create Conspiracy	Value is Established
Person A has no personal agenda prior to the action.	The position of principal opens.	"I *do not know* what will happen."	Evidence is gathered.	Nothing happens.	Outcome is perceived as positive, negative or neutral.

Figure 13.2.

PRACTICAL ADVICE

Do the research.

It certainly takes time to investigate, but better to place the emphasis on the front end than to spend countless hours repairing one's character on the back. Likewise, just as you probably do not make hustled decisions when planning the events of your life, career, and so forth, try not to assume that the administration rushes to judgment either. In other words, allow the facts to surface prior to the assumption that the suits have it out for us.

Neutral is awesome!

There will be times when events occur in a school, and it will be difficult to reserve judgment. However, those who allow themselves the option of viewing an event without a personal connection seem to be less stressed. Just because something happens does not mean that we have to enter into the fray. It is okay to step aside (like when we hear the ambulance siren) and allow others to work out their issues without our interference or opinions.

FOR THE CLASSROOM

Judge the actions, not the child.

Although this timeless adage goes without saying, we work in emotional environments. In times of stress, it is easy to place the heat on the child instead of the action. We all make mistakes and the hope is that the mistakes our children make will make them less prone to making the same ones in adulthood. It is appropriate to hold students accountable, but do it with the dignity and respect that you would want for your own child.

Share the message.

In addition to our dictated curriculum, we also relay to our students many lessons that speak to leadership and character. Many student conflicts are born through the actions of the conspiracy theorist. By teaching this concept to students, perhaps we can limit the damage that occurs when we judge without evidence. Plus, the concept of securing proof runs parallel to many of our standard assignments. Recall Coach Browning's advice in chapter 9.

NOTE

1. Fienberg, W., & Soltis J. F. (1998). *School and society*. New York: Teachers College Press.

FOURTEEN

The Closer the Better

Suppose you were right in the middle of an argument between people with two different political opinions. Notwithstanding your affiliation (for this example, please see yourself as neutral), let's suppose each was trying to gain favor.

Bill and John argue constantly. This week, the topic is centered on failing school districts. Bill believes that we need to provide more funding to failing schools. He sees their failure as a letdown of the system. Bill does not judge their flaws as isolated, but as a reflection of government as well.

John, on the other hand, has taken a different view. John wants less money to go to failing schools. He believes that these schools should be held accountable for their failure and sees it as government's responsibility to fix the situation if the school leadership cannot.

If we start to think about how this argument would proceed, picture yourself sitting at a table with Bill on one side of you and John on the other. In such a format, each would be able to present information to point out their thoughts while also counting their opponents'. This format is fairly typical, and victory usually resides in the opinions of the witnesses.

Much of society utilizes debate to solve conflict. From court cases to street disagreements, people try to convince each other of their points by defining the benefits of their position. For example, perhaps Bill could mention how a particular school turned their achievement around through a government grant; conversely, maybe John could mention how the government takeover of another school helped to raise its test scores. In each example, sharing one's success could be seen as a way to increase support.

73

Additionally, people sometimes look to gather backing by dismantling their opponent's tenets using negative campaigns. For instance, in Bill's case, perhaps disclosing the many times government has tried to hold schools accountable and failed could be a useful tactic. Conversely, maybe John could tally the millions of dollars that have already been "misused" assisting failing schools. Perhaps that number could sway a few votes to his side?

Does this form of argument seem familiar? It should be, for most of the world argues in this fashion. *However, what if this format were exactly what one should* not *do in trying to garner favor of the masses? Could this thinking even be possible?*

Although a foreign concept, perhaps the greatest way to influence is to start with the opposition's tenets. In other words, the better we are at coming closer to our adversary, the better the chance at having a neutral party move to our way of thinking.

Consider figure 14.1. If the masses sit in an unbiased position at the center of the argument, the more one person argues individual points, the more he moves "away" from the safety of the center. Here is where consensus lies. In other words, the more Bill argues for his viewpoint, the less people will be willing to move away from center (safety).

This line of thinking stems from understanding that agreement has depth and breadth. According to Clabaugh and Rozycki, depth measures how strong the agreement is (how much we really agree), and breadth measures how many folks agree (the number).[1] The more we move away from our opponent, the less people (breadth) will agree with us, but with more intensity in their agreement.

There are numerous occurrences where consensus is limited by how we decide to handle a situation. Just as many folks may support the idea of having safe schools, placing metal detectors at the front door may not be agreeable to people. In this example, we can see that consensus (the number of people in agreement) starts to wane when we actually decide to do something (pick an action).

Experts in consensus research may contend that this concept asks people to water down their argument or perhaps making their argument devoid of substance (talk in generalities; limit actions). For instance, it is much easier to say to someone, "I see your point" and do nothing than it

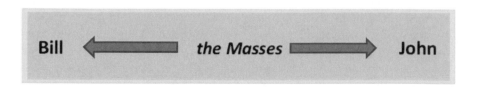

Figure 14.1.   Moving Away from Neutral

is to negotiate the right action to take in a given situation. Yet, this is not the basis of this discourse.

In schools, we deal with human beings and a litany of possible ways that "problems" can and should be solved. *In schools, absolute opposites do not necessarily exist.* For instance, one reading specialist may feel that we need to work on fluency, another may select reading strategies; however, neither is an absolute opposite of the other, and thus, selecting just one would limit the possibility for success. People may have different opinions, but when we closely examine their ideas and the possibilities of success, we must come to realize that either way may get the job done — and done well.

Defining successful outcomes is the basis for understanding, cooperation, and possible consensus. Often times, though, we neglect to establish this root in clear terms. For instance, the less we can articulate what a failing and/or successful school is, the more difficult it will be to select measures to "fix" perceived problems.

Moving closer to the antithesis establishes the premise that all possibilities are indeed possible. In seeing the opportunities, and clearly defining outcomes, we create a less stressful situation for all of us, especially in what is supposed to be a cooperative, congenial environment. Once more, those who habitually try to convince others of their point by going directly against their opponent make it difficult for the masses to follow them. Since issues have width and depth, the more we argue for the opposite of what we believe, the more we become the opposite of our initial intentions. To truly persuade others, we must move in the opposite direction of where our instincts tell us to go.

PRACTICAL ADVICE

No one wins a fight.

Sound advice from my fifth grade PE teacher Mr. Westerfield and still relevant today. In building relationships, fighting serves to define the powerful and powerless. Yet, the nature of sustaining relationships must allow disagreement without desertion, conflict without conquest. People may argue; folks can disagree. But ultimately, we must create relationships that see the value of compromise by surrendering the desire to always be correct.

Define the end game.

Since many issues of culture revolve around compromise (defining what is right for the situation), we must be clear in defining successful outcomes. Failure to state the end game creates chaos and a host of assertions as to what is right. As teachers, we must understand that winning starts and ends with children. It is this simple motto that will keep us focused on the successful results of our profession.

FOR THE CLASSROOM

Come closer to students.

Every opportunity we have with children places us in a unique and powerful position of influence. Every child is not necessarily going to be our favorite, but every child deserves the same opportunity as the next, despite their dispositions. Although some children can really challenge our thinking, authority, and so forth, we must strive not to take their actions as personal affronts against us. Remember, nobody wins a fight. Look for ways to compromise with compassion. Remember, we do not give up authority by avoiding confrontations.

Teach this concept.

What a wonderful world this might be if everyone started by appreciating each other's position on issues. When relaying lessons of grammar or molecules, be sure to add this lesson to your repertoire of best-practice strategies. Although not concurrent with typical persuasive strategies, teaching your students to see the value of their opponent may just build a more accepting cultural environment for all.

Remember, when dealing with human beings, culture (the way we do things) is negotiated; therefore, without a correct route, success can be found in varied views. Think about it—even a GPS gives options.

NOTE

1. Clabaugh, K. G., & Rozycki, G. E. (1990). *Understanding schools: The foundations of education.* New York: Harper and Row.

FIFTEEN

Don't Bite the Boss!

You wanted to be the teacher. You took countless courses, spent the money, did the time. You went through interview after interview, and you finally got the job. Congratulations! You did it. All that hard work paid off. But wait a minute. Think for a moment. Besides you, what other person do you owe a hand of gratitude? What other person most likely went through every interview with you? Spoke on your behalf? Shook your hand when you finally got the job. Well?

Just as you did a ton of work to get to this point, so did your boss. Consider this, when the committee was trying to decide on the final candidate, do you think your boss was in your corner? Chances are, the boss saw something in you that said you would be a great fit. Perhaps it was your compassion for students or your passionate enthusiasm or your commitment to results. Whatever the reasons, the boss wanted you, and now that you have the job, you are a part of the team—the team that the boss put together. So what is the issue?

As a teacher, your "employees" are the students. Despite the fact that we cannot select whom we teach, we can certainly think about it. What type of students would you want in your classroom? What qualities would you want them to possess? Would you want students who worked hard, were good teammates, and had compassion for others? Or would you want a rebel—a real hooligan whose concern for you and the class was nonexistent?

When it comes to the hiring process, principals are not looking for drones; they are searching for teammates. Just as you would want students who cooperate, so too does your boss.

It is amazing how many people forget this concept when they get the job. It is like they become the classroom guru and all bets are off when it comes to team. The same teachers who become infuriated when students demonstrate a disrespectful attitude are the very same folks who mock the principal for being incompetent or nonexistent. But why?

Your *team, as a teacher, must include* your *boss.* Period. You are the teacher; but the boss is still responsible for more in the organization. Cutting the boss out of the team only results in bitter feelings and distrust, which can lead to reprimands or worse.

Therefore, it is not all right to make fun of your boss in public or through e-mail. It is not all right to blame the office for every woe of the school. It is not all right to set up an "us versus them" mentality when it comes to the office and the classroom. Got it? *Teachers, who consistently present the office as the enemy wind up teaching somewhere else.*

In being an educator, we want to be confident in what we are doing, but not cocky. If you fell into a black hole on the way to work, the school would open. The kids would learn, and we would find a new teacher. Don't play God. Appreciate what you have while you have it.

Don't bite the boss. Follow this simple maxim during your tenure, and chances are you will have a very successful stay.

PRACTICAL ADVICE

When you disagree, do it in private.

It is okay to disagree with your boss, but it is foolish to fight a public battle. When you have a disagreement, talk about it. Reason with each other (if possible). Once that time passes, it is incumbent upon you to be a good team player. Remember, would you want a student to stand up in class and blatantly challenge you?

Find someone you can complain to outside of your district.

Use your husband or wife. Find a colleague somewhere far away that you really trust. If you simply cannot take it and have to complain about your boss, do it with someone outside of your school system. "These walls have ears" (Dionysius of Syracuse). Likewise, if you were hired prior to your boss, give her a chance to earn your respect. Limit the conspiracies and judge the actions without assuming intent.

FOR THE CLASSROOM

Practice the same with your students.

Here, you are the boss. Be sure to afford your students the very same opportunities you would want from your boss. Be respectful. Agree with enthusiasm; disagree with assurance. Offer genuine conversations. Let it be known that it is okay to differ in an appropriate manner. People want to be heard—so listen well.

Watch your speech patterns.

Remember, the classroom belongs to everyone. Be wary of personal and possessive pronouns. Saying "our" classroom instead of "my" classroom goes a long way! Establish a collaborative community by modeling genuine respect and dignity for all. Plus, blasting the boss to students is unprofessional. Keep your dirty laundry out of the classroom. Nobody wins a fight.

VI

Systems Thinking

*VARIATIONS, AND OUR ACCEPTANCE OR DENIAL OF THEM,
CAUSE THE EBB AND FLOW OF THE HUMAN TIDE.*

SIXTEEN

"Say It Ain't So, Joe."

September 28, 1920.

Do you know this date? Any guesses? Supposedly, this is the day that "Shoeless" Joe Jackson, an iconic baseball player for the Chicago White Sox, admitted to taking a bribe during the World Series to help the Cincinnati Reds win the championship. The quote, "Say it ain't so, Joe," was apparently murmured by a young fan at the time, distraught over the news of his fallen hero.[1]

Much has been written about the Sox scandal, and in fact, there have even been movies made about it. These tales call into question our understanding of ethics, value judgments, power, and a slew of other issues.

As Shoeless Joe Jackson's name has become known over the years, a sure bet may be that the name Joe Frost has not. Joe Frost's story brings an interesting twist to not only Jackson's legacy, but to the teaching profession at large.

Joe Frost was a decorated naval mechanic who was now "working" during his retirement. (Funny how in today's world retirement seldom means retiring.) Joe was currently a beach tag vender in Sea Isle, New Jersey. His job was to stand at the entrance to the beach and check beach tags. Pretty simple stuff, especially for a guy who was used to securing nuclear submarines.

"Check the tags for the adults. If a person does not have a tag, sell them one. Otherwise, they cannot go onto the beach." The parting words from his immediate supervisor before his inaugural shift resonated. Joe was a man of detail, and he always followed instructions from his superiors. Perfection was the norm, particularly from his days dealing with atomic artillery.

Joe started out his morning in superior fashion. Two families arrived at the beach, had their tags, and thanked him for his hearty "good morning."

"Seems like I made the right decision," he thought to himself. It feels good when you have success, especially when you are new. However, that success was very, very short lived.

The next family to show up was the Kennedys. They owned a house right across the street from the beach. Spacious and expensive. The type of place one drives by and thinks, "What do they do for a living?" Anyway, before Joe could give his now standard, "Good morning, folks," Mrs. Kennedy interrupted and asked about the whereabouts of Alice, the former tag person who had been at this post for the last decade. Joe knew nothing of Alice and tried to explain that he was new. But that didn't seem to matter to Mrs. Kennedy. She ignored his retort and made a beeline for the stairs. At that, Joe politely asked if she had her beach tag.

Needless to say, Mrs. Kennedy did not take kindly to being questioned. In fact, she exploded like a Mark 45 torpedo aimed straight at Joe's head. Her assault on Joe lasted a good three minutes. (That might not seem like a lot of time, but count down from 10 slowly . . . 10, 9, 8 . . . . Get the point? Now times that by 18!) From the "You're being ridiculous," to "My children are sweating," Mrs. Kennedy went on and on.

Her major complaint dealt with Joe himself. You see, Joe was not Alice, the regular beach tag lady. Alice had stood guard at that entrance to the beach for over a decade. She knew the families. She knew the families' families. In fact, she knew everyone. And in knowing everyone, she knew the Kennedys (Who wouldn't?). She knew that they were "good for" the beach tags, as Mr. Kennedy always showed up on Sundays with the tags pinned to his trunks.

Joe, however, did not know the Kennedys (and about this time, wished he had never met them). Joe also did not know the Walbers, the Fowlmans, or the Billingsons either. Joe had no context for relationships. He had no sense of being "good for something." But Joe knew beach tags. And he knew if you didn't have one, you weren't getting onto the beach.

As one can imagine, it was a long day for Joe, and even a longer wait for folks to find their tags. No one was happy. Not Joe or the Walbers or the Kennedys (not surprising). But guess who else wasn't happy? Joe's boss, who on the second day of Joe's employment, phoned Alice and asked if she would consider taking her spot back for one more season. She agreed. As it turns out, Joe was not cut out for the beach tag business. Too stressful.

As mentioned earlier, there are certain similarities between Joe Frost and Joe Jackson. Besides the fact that neither wore shoes on the job, both Joes lost in the court of public opinion. However, what makes this parallel so intriguing is that they lost by *doing the exact opposite* in terms of moral decisions.

Joe Jackson's offense is more evident. He cheated. Although skepticism reigns high, as his batting average and fielding were impeccable during the series, he was attached to purposefully losing, a huge NO in the eyes of the masses. Jackson let his teammates, the owners, and the fans down, and for that, his legacy will live in infamy as a member of the "Black Sox" scandal.

Joe Frost has a legacy too, but the more positive one is known at a naval base on the Islands. Joe also lost in the eyes of the people; however, his defeat actually came at the expense of his practiced morality. Again, Joe was a man of precision and ethics. He could not just "let" people on the beach without paying for tags. That just wouldn't do. Beaches had to be watched; boardwalks cleaned, and public employees paid. Letting one slide only causes havoc to the system, which is designed with dos and don'ts.

Joe Frost's crime is not in his decision to check beach tags. In fact, Joe did not commit a crime at all. He did his job and did it well. The problem arises when discrepancy and interpretation are allowed to enter into systems that on the surface seem exact, but when you peel away the shell, reveal a new layer of complexity.

Now, you may be wondering, what does this story have to do with teaching and school systems? The answer resides in our understanding that "the system" is people. Wherever people interact within a given society, the mannerism in which they interact can vary. These variations, and our acceptance or denial of them, cause the ebb and flow of the human tide.

For example, does your school have a policy for gum chewing? Chewing gum, on the surface, is not a huge deal. Yes, it is understood the maintenance people may get upset, and also realize there will be students who may abuse the privilege—blow bubbles, chew loudly. But as far as school discipline goes, there are far worse offenses than enjoying a slice of sugar cane and beet juice.

But the concealed agenda of gum chewing has to do with power, control, and in this scenario, discretion. Suppose you are a teacher who does not allow students to chew gum. Now, let us also suppose your teammate does. Who is right? Who is correct? If it is a school rule, then technically, you would be correct. You would be "justified" in writing the discipline referrals each time some snarly little rascal hunkered down on his Hubba Bubba. And yet, I wonder what the office would think of you, day after day, processing gum-chewing referrals while other serious incidents persisted?

You would be justified in being upset with the principals if they shunned your actions. It is pretty difficult to have students understand that coming from Mrs. So and So's class, where they are allowed to "break the rules," does not give them the right to chew gum in yours. Likewise, wonder what the kids think of you? It would not be farfetched to believe that you might be the center of attention at lunchtime (and not for good reasons). And yet, here is where the metamorphosis commences. You are now Joe Frost, doing the correct thing, and suffering in the public's eyes. Say it ain't so!

But behold your partner. She does not escape blame either. To her colleagues, she is Shoeless Joe (or Clueless). She is throwing the rest of the teachers under the school bus by not following the rules. Sure, the kids might love her, but even that is a short-lived benefit when she has no one to sit with at faculty meetings.

Now do not get all dejected and think there is no solution. There is, and it lies in the fact that there is no single solution. We need to understand that *sometimes perfect isn't always right*. In dealing with human beings, subtle and not so subtle interpretations of culture (how we do things) can lead to varying results. And yet, we cannot look upon these differences as judgments toward us or how we do what we do.

Variations of culture are not meant to thwart the noble acts of another. They just are. It is our ability (or nonability) to handle these situations in the short and long term that set the tone for not only our class, but also our careers.

PRACTICAL ADVICE

Teachers burn out because they cannot control the variations.

As a teacher, you are not in a position to discipline your colleagues. And even though you may desire the administration to "catch" them, spending your time wishing that "they get theirs" is exhausting. Is it okay to let the principal know people are letting things go? Yes. It is. But after, we need to move ahead.

Sometimes doing the correct thing is a lonely task.

If you pride yourself on your conviction follow to the rules, than by all means, you have the right to follow them. But understand, you may be prone to Joe Frost syndrome. For example, if a teacher who did not manage student behavior well was replaced by an LTS who held students accountable for their actions and work, he/she may not win the "most popular teacher" award. On the surface, that should be okay. But we are all human beings. And even the hardest of the hard cares about perception. Replacing ineffectiveness with effectiveness may cause stormy waters at first. Over time, though, these seas will subside.

FOR THE CLASSROOM

Offer alternatives to ultimatums.

Should Joe Frost have allowed people to go onto the beach without a tag? That's a tough call. It worked for Alice, but she had context. Should you allow students to chew gum? Get a pencil when they didn't bring one? Turn in a missing assignment late? The sure money might be on establishing a system that works for you *and the students*. For example, you do not lose your house the first time you make a late payment on your mortgage. Right? In fact, you do not lose it on the second, or third, or fourth, and so forth. It takes a while. One does not "let students slide" by affording them the same treatment adults receive "in the real world." Bean counters burn out fast! And 30 years is a heck of a lot longer than 10, 9, 8, times 18!

Model lifelong learning with your grading.

Revising is a strategy that increases determination and "stick-to-itive-ness." Likewise, anxiety lessens when students know they will genuinely have an opportunity to learn for knowledge rather than just the grade. Sure, standardized tests are not set up that way, but the classrooms are not standardized. (We can teach and assess the standards, but affording students multiple opportunities to truly master a standard is how we make the difference when the standardized assessment counts.) By designing a structure that takes the grade out of the main focus, we set the target at learning versus attaining just a mark.

Allow students to revise essays or retake assessments to ensure they have really learned the material. You may have to vary the assignment, but better ensure that learning has occurred while in our control than to notice it has not on the next state assessment.

NOTE

1. Gropman, D. (1979). *Say it ain't so, Joe!: The true story of Shoeless Joe Jackson*. New York: Kensington Publishing Corporation.

SEVENTEEN
What's the Win?

Consider this situation:

Let's say that you have a student (Roberta) in your eighth grade classroom who is in need of math tutoring. You are her math teacher and Roberta has approached you before for assistance. In the past, you were not able to assist students after school because your babysitter was not available. Now, having secured child care, you are ready to begin tutoring again; yet, times have changed since your last undertaking.

In pursuit of helping Roberta, you run into an entanglement between the union and the central office when it comes to the correct amount for compensation. The district is holding tight to the contract language that states it is 40 dollars an hour for tutoring; however, the union believes that the hour is worth 50 dollars, as was the new precedent that was set forth this past year during summer school. Both the union and the office have asked you to give them a day or two to rectify the situation.

Two weeks have gone by since your request with no resolution. Now what?

In being a member of the union, certainly you would not want to go against the cause. Likewise, 10 bucks is 10 bucks! Although that dollar amount won't break the bank, every little bit helps, especially when it comes to paying for child-care needs. In addition, one would not want to upset central office. Although not a formal directive, interfering with this situation could be seen as meddling, thus potentially hurting one's reputation.

In any given situation, it is wise to consider both sides of the argument. However, despite your alliance to both entities, the ultimate win is for the child to attain the appropriate educational support. Even though there are other issues at play—ones that happen to be out of your juris-diction—what is in your control is searching for an alternative.

Perhaps there is someone who offers sessions during lunch or maybe during a breakfast club. Maybe there is a high school student who would be willing to assist. In not wanting to "bite the boss" or compound the issue for the union, your opinion here may not be part of a viable solution on either end.

In considering wins, we must allow our brains to go beyond *what is* to see *what needs to be*. We cannot be pulled into battles that detract us from the goal of winning for the students—our ultimate mission. But it is a delicate balance to negotiate when you are dealing with special interest groups vying for resources, attention, and so forth.

One of the greatest strategists who ever walked our earth was the Chinese philosopher Sun Tzu. In his book entitled *The Art of War*, he stated, "For to win one hundred victories in one hundred battles is not the acme of skill. To subdue the enemy without fighting is the acme of skill."[1]

In educational terms, to enter into every scholastic skirmish only exhausts our efforts and leaves us depleted for when they truly matter.

WINNING IS NOT DEFINED BY THE ARGUMENT; IT IS DEFINED BY THE NONARGUMENT BUT STILL ACCOMPLISHING THE SAME RESULTS.

In considering our opening scenario, winning is getting the student what she needs; everything else is someone else's campaign. Can you have an opinion? Sure. Give it when asked, but to enter the fray just to be right or just because you are close to the situation is impulsive and unwise. Do not exhaust yourself with every wrangle that comes your way. Be smart and exercise your right to pass.

As teachers, we sit in a position of power. And that power comes with responsibility to ourselves, the team, and the students and families. But power can be a funny thing. Power can be used to break down walls or build impenetrable forces. The goal for us must be to utilize our position to avoid the conflict but still attain the desired outcome. To accomplish this mission, sometimes we are going to win, and sometimes it will require us to lose. (Yes, it is okay to lose in leadership.)

Knowing when to lose is the mark of ingenuity.

One way to determine your course of action when it comes to defining the win can start by considering this simple, but effective, proposal—*What is best for this child?* As you explore the possible answer to this question, difficult situations will start to become clear about the actions you should or should not take. As a teacher, you will have various vantage points from which people will try to convince you to see "their" win. Stay firm to your central mission and always remember why we are here.

What is best for this *child?*

PRACTICAL ADVICE

Sometimes planned failures are a good thing.

In considering the ultimate win for a child, there may be times when personal loss can provide a better win for the over-all communication. For instance, maybe finding a lunch tutor will work in this circumstance. Although you may lose out on the extra cash, the child gets the help, and you get the satisfaction of knowing all is well.

Don't hesitate to ask for help.

Mentioned previously, the greatest resource we have in the education business is people. Be sure to utilize the whole team if necessary to secure a win for a student. Galaxies of possibilities exist seconds away so long as we forgo the need to control everything. Furthermore, look to place yourself in an assistive role. Others may have issues and possible answers. Help them focus upon the students.

FOR THE CLASSROOM

Always be steadfast in your primary function.

If you are a Spanish teacher, be sure your planning and actions reflect that end. Too often, we become sidetracked by other initiatives or agendas. Student achievement is our goal; we must look to develop our students in various ways. However, we must still follow the standards and teach the curriculum. Those who are "great listeners" or "wonderful mentors" but neglect the curriculum needs are doing a disservice to the students.

Do not solve issues; present possibilities.

In teaching students to be critical thinkers and problem solvers, we must suppress our wanting to solve issues for students. This is not to say that giving sound advice is not warranted. It is, but present the information in a scenario format. This way, you allow the students to see "the win" from their (and other) vantage points. Match the need with possible winning situations. Create thinking and learning opportunities.

NOTE

1. Tzu, Sun. (1910). *The art of war*. (L. Giles, Trans.). London: Department of Oriental Printed Books and MSS in the British Museum.

EIGHTEEN

Compared to What

James Van Persie presented one of his favorite scenarios to his class:

"You have decided to celebrate the week's end by going out to dinner at a great restaurant. For the purposes of this decision, please select the restaurant of your choice that fits this description. Please be sure to explain why this restaurant is great. *In other words, define the factors that make it so."*

James Van Persie's purpose was to jolt a lively conversation in his leadership class on the topic of negotiating. He had given this assignment before and was used to chatting about burgers and barbecue. However, as each group responded with a bistro and basis, what became clear was something he had never experienced—each group selected a reason other than food.

Previously, the assumption and responses of his classes had been consistent. Prior students connected "great" to food. But this class was different. This class associated the word "great" to define the means (service, parking, and price) to enable the end (enjoying the food). This class leveraged the outcome on the assumption that if other aspects of the restaurant were not great prior to eating, then the meal would not ascend to such heights.

As Mr. P pondered the results after class, he could not help but think he had reached a new level in his search for higher-order thinking. The entire notion of "great" was now in question. Needless to say, he could not wait until tomorrow's class!

How do we know something is "great"? This timeless philosophical question stems from the depths of time and logic, but still poses no definitive answer. Much of our value system that is inherent in us is built upon context and exposure. *Everything in life is compared to what.* As one first reads this statement, it would be easy to see its initial position as a question; however, to view it as such would limit its true meaning. Context—

the conditions surrounding an event, thinking, situation, and so forth—offers the individual a barometer for analysis.

For instance, suppose you were the head coach of a school soccer team in the D division. Your regular season consists of competing against other D divisional teams, and the top three teams make it to the district playoffs. If your team made it to the playoffs, would you consider it to be a successful season? What if in the playoffs, you had to compete against C teams, in which case you lost miserably. Would this still have been a successful season?

The answers to the latter questions are built upon the context of the initial situation. In order to define success, we must be able to measure it against other instances of success that position its intent in relation to what is possible. In other words, if D division has less skilled players than C division, it would be reasonable to assume D teams would lose to C teams, thus providing a framework for judgment. The advent of favorites and underdogs is derived from situations like this.

(As a side note, it is always interesting when mentioning underdogs to reference what I call *Julius Caesar Syndrome*. Briefly, what we must understand is that the "mob is fickle," as Caesar learned all too late. As long as the favorite in any situation remains the favorite, folks often desire them to falter. This phenomenon may have something to do with our nature of believing that everyone should have their day in the sun. Rarely do folks want the perennial powerhouse to continue to be successful unless they are part [player, fan, etc.] of that team. This is just an observation, but one worth citing.)

As human beings, we consistently look to define ourselves against standards of what is. Hair commercials, clothing ads, and the like all look to establish a norm from which judgments can be made. But what we often fail to establish is a baseline for what we define as "normal" or "good." In simple terms, we can perceive that D division is not as skilled as C division based upon a defined set of skills, but without the understanding of what we consider to be a successful season, our standard becomes defined by what has been instead of what could be.

For example, what if the D divisional team was last year's E division winner? What if this team was undefeated in the league and won every game in the playoffs en route to a championship? Might a successful D season be winning half the games?

Context has such a place in life, yet sometimes we fail to define the conditions for success prior to entering the game. In a sense, we are judged by the known standard and not necessarily the one that has the proper context for our situation. ("Gosh! That D team stinks. They only won six games.") This scenario plays out in schools all the time!

Just as there are different opinions on what makes for a great restaurant (food, location, parking, service), so too reside a host of characteristics that define a great teacher, a great lesson, a great student. As stated before, our brains want to make connections. We find comfort in defining people, situations, conflicts, and so forth. Here, the aspect of order comes into play. Yet, it is difficult to know every circumstance surrounding the daily lives of those around us. Just as it may seem apparent (and recommended) to be on time for work, are there situations that provide a different context in which it may be necessary to be late? Of course!

As teachers, we use comparisons constantly. From year to year and class to class, comparisons are being made. As students experience different teachers with different approaches to teaching, reputations are built upon the experiences of the students. For example, if there are 300 students in a particular grade, the number of teachers can vary. In each experience of a grade, both students and parents make comparisons. In this instance, practices are judged by uniformity. ("Mrs. Smith's class took a field trip, how come our class did not?")

Within this scenario, the new competition can become consistency. In other words, so as not to "outshine" others, we succumb to comparing ourselves to another standard. We all know people who do because they want to be noticed. This line of thinking is flawed; and these folks should be avoided for their insecurities breed jealousy and contempt. Yet, those who dim their own worth so as not to place another person under the bar should also be questioned.

In our profession, we must establish a consensus about what we define as successful outcomes based on what we are hired to do. Certainly, the instructions of the standards, along with the various best-practice strategies are of value, and should be mandated as our primary curricular function. But as teachers of human beings, there is so much more to be known, shared, compared, and defined.

How do we know something is great? The answer resides in our definition of great and the agreement (or non-agreement) of outcomes that make it so. Realizing the duality of this concept (knowing what is not great and being able to define it) allows us to establish instructional, social, intellectual, and the like, norms for comparison.

PRACTICAL ADVICE

Observe other teachers.

The student body may feel that you are the greatest teacher since Aristotle, but without a clearly defined context of what they know (content), we have not challenged ourselves to move beyond the assumed known. See other teachers teach. Take the good and the bad. Make comparisons. Define what works for you, for them, and ultimately, what will work for the students. The more we learn of ourselves in relation to what exists outside of what we know, the more we can stretch and grow.

Solicit critical feedback.

If you have the type of administrator who tells you everything is hunky-dory, perhaps it is time to invite a colleague in for real feedback. In other words, if the D division teams only play E divisions, they will never have the opportunity to stretch the possibilities of performance. It is okay not to be great at everything. Lifelong learning is everywhere! Take it upon yourself to know what you do not know. Test your thinking. Make change and try anew.

FOR THE CLASSROOM

Use rubrics.

Providing the standard for success is no longer a good idea, but a necessity. Context must be present, for when the conditions for success are readily defined, the odds increase for students to reach lofty zeniths. Furthermore, just using a rubric is not enough. We must take the time to explain each domain with definable examples to provide the grounds for success.

Model your work for them.

Visual learning is such a powerful tool. When students can see your work, it provides a standard for success and affirms that the assignment is of value. Although student-to-student modeling works, nothing conveys the importance of an assignment like witnessing the teacher performing the same act. Although it may take more time, the investment is well worth the return on the initial assignment, but also on building a culture of respect, motivation, and success. "I do. We do. You do."

VII

Now and Zen

THE ONLY SECURE THING IN LIFE IS THAT WE ARE ALL INSECURE.

NINETEEN

13.1

Think about the last time someone was proud of you. Can you recall the specific details of the event? Perhaps you earned a certain degree that had taken a long and tedious process to complete. Or maybe you finally got over your fear of the ocean and took a plunge with the kids. Or maybe you and your family took that risk you had been avoiding for years and purchased that vacation home after all. Needless to say, these events, like the ones in your life, can be treasured milestones and a source for feeling good about ourselves and our accomplishments. Yet, perhaps this historical pattern of linking self-esteem with actions could be doing more damage than good, especially for our children.

Buddy Burros was a tremendous football player. In fact, the whole town of Carlsberg knew from the moment Buddy put cleats on that he was going to be something special. It all started prior to his birth. Buddy's dad, Buddy Sr., happened to be a state champion in track and field and was captain of the varsity football team in high school and college. His mother, Sonia, was a tremendous athlete in her own right. A three-time tennis champion, she was certainly one of the most prolific female sports personalities ever to champion the Carlsberg's courts.

Buddy was an only child and from day one was bred to be a champion. From the summer camps to seasonal workouts, Buddy was busy becoming a star. And a star was exactly what he was on the gridiron. In fact, during his first official football game (he was six years old; the other students were nine), Buddy scored seven touchdowns. Seven!

As the years went by, his statistics grew, and so too did the legend of Buddy Burros. High school scouts would watch him in grade school; college scouts would visit high school. And there were even professional football spies vying for his "unofficial" attention. No matter what the situation, Buddy was the center of

*interest and the pride of Carlsberg . . . until his ruptured his Achilles tendon
during a pickup basketball game with a few friends.*

*Needless to say, the injury was devastating to not only Buddy, but the entire
town. Legend has it that folks at Grafters café actually cried when they heard the
news. Sure, Buddy went through rehabilitation and did his best to make a come-
back, but unfortunately, the damage was done. He had lost a step, and with it,
sank into the realm of mediocrity.*

*Buddy, now a father of three, looks back upon his time as a "football star"
with indifference. His sons, all soccer players, hardly know the story of Buddy's
legend, and that is the way Buddy wants it to be. Memories, like scars, remain
even after they have healed.*

The story of Buddy Burros is not meant to create sadness but to supply us
with a contextual framework for this discussion. There are countless athletes who succumb to career-ending injuries and suffer through the emotions of loss and regret. But what causes the ultimate sadness may not
necessarily be the injury itself, but the emotional void. Such is the case
when we associate self-worth with actions.

Why do so many children have self-esteem issues? We, as educators
and parents, know the pattern all too well. Comparisons are made about
who is pretty or intelligent. Standards are set, and dreams are built and
dashed based upon the impact of our attaining such traits. Yet, with all of
these known traps, the hidden self-esteem issue unfortunately is perpetu-
ated by us.

As adults, we do not look to create esteem issues in our children. In
fact, we are constantly looking for ways to support a healthy self-image.
We do this by praising accomplishments. However, it is the very practice
that we employ that may be contributing to low self-worth.

For example, Buddy Sr. was proud of his son. He told him so every
time he scored a touchdown or made an incredible play of defense. But
unfortunately, the phrase "I am proud of you" only followed an accomplishment (an action deemed as successful). Such praise was not stated
just for Buddy.

When we attach praise (pride) to a successful action, we are subcon-
sciously telling our children that self-worth is contingent upon accomplishments and not just for the person. This consistent reinforcement
creates children who, in looking to secure their self-image, search to find
the next thing they can do to be deemed a success.

If students start to attribute successful actions as pride-building experiences, then to think that failing actions counter the successes is not so
foreign a concept. Fear has a tremendous place in this discussion. Fear of
rejection, failure, and so forth can cripple folks when it comes to trying
something new, moving forward. Yet, perhaps the attachment of pride to
actions is contributing to the growing amount of pressure and fear our
students feel day in and day out.

Seem absurd? Think about how many students over the years have been scared to try, tentative to contribute. We realize that building safe risk taking is paramount for student success, and yet, many of our practices reward successful actions without much concern for the whole child.

Emotional intelligence research identifies significant factors of student achievement that had been previously thought of as "sentimental fluff."[1] Yet, as we develop our understanding of the concept that self-image impacts learning, we must be diligent in studying our practices to ensure we are not continuing the very pattern of fear and low self-esteem that we have affirmed as detrimental to our children.

Critics of this line of thinking sometimes believe that we are doing a disservice to students by building their hopes up when the reality of a situation would dictate failure. For instance, should five-year-olds receive a trophy at a sporting event for participating? There are many folks who believe this practice is "destroying" the youth of America by continuing the fabrication that everyone is a winner. Yet, we must ask ourselves this question—if we do not reward risk taking at an early age, when do we believe children will be comfortable to try new experiences?

In judging the practice of rewarding for participation, we must also ask ourselves this critical question—who put this practice into motion? Certainly, the young athletes could not have secured the resources to do so. Indeed, it was their parents. Why? The assumption that they are trying to avoid the hurt to their children that the parents experienced in their youth is not far-fetched. As parents, that is what we do.

The title of this chapter is "13.1." Do you have any guess as to its significance? This is the exact distance of a half marathon—13.1 miles. Now ask yourself another question—why are there half marathons? Are there finish lines? Do people cheer? This critical inquiry hopefully sheds light upon the original premise.

To truly win, do we have all have to run 26.2 miles?

PRACTICAL ADVICE

Happy, not proud.

The next time someone shares with you a successful accomplishment, be sure to tell them you are happy for them, but you are proud of who she is. Separating actions from building self-image may just be the start of securing a healthy approach to the endless comparisons this world places upon the unassuming.

Share this idea.

Inevitably, when you first start to utilize this change in your speech pattern, folks will ask you what is going on. Be sure to take your time and explain the rationale behind the change in perspective and practice. Whether a person wins or loses does not matter in building a sustainable strength to try.

FOR THE CLASSROOM

Be wary of grades.

In realizing that grades are a part of our culture in the educational system, we must look for ways to encourage extended learning. Encouraged internal motivation leads to self-actualization and a deeper appreciation of accomplishment (the process of trying). One such practice that enables students to start from a position of power is to give them all A's and ask that they work to ensure the grade rather than working from a zero staring point. In realizing that this is not an easy proposition, your simple awareness of this position may just be enough to redesign lessons with a focus on choice and rewarding the process and much as the product.

Differentiate.

Although easier said than done, your ability to meet students on their level of experience and learning will make all the difference in fostering a spirit of inquisitiveness. Safe risk taking takes into account instructing students on a level that meets their educational prowess. Build in opportunities for your students to feel confident in trying based upon the precursor to success—fostering a sense of "I can do this."

We cannot control winning, but we can control our effort.

NOTE

1. Goleman, Daniel. (1995). *Emotional intelligence: Why It can matter more than IQ.* New York: Bantam.

TWENTY

The Burden of Hope

Melinda Carver was a superb family and consumer science (FCS) instructor. Her lessons were built upon the standards, were always real-world applicable, and took into account students' cultural backgrounds. Her observations were always stellar, and her dedication to her students was second to none.

However, despite her efforts, Lincoln High School was going through budget reductions, and FCS was a subject that was being discussed as a possible cut. Needless to say, Melinda took the realization of a possible layoff with great concern.

On the day of the decision, FCS was spared, and everyone, including Melinda, was tremendously happy . . . until the next spring when the cut conversations started again.

And as one might have expected, FCS was on the hot list again. Unfortunately for the members of this department, this routine continued for several years. Each spring, FCS teachers would sit in the school board meeting awaiting the news. Although freed from termination, the entire process took its toll on the staff's morale. "It is difficult to stay positive when you continually feel undervalued." These sentiments were echoed by teachers and supporters alike.

Melinda, however, was of a different breed. Although she too was saddened by future possibilities, she also saw each decision as one more chance to "make that difference" in a child's life. As the other teachers were lamenting about what could be, Melinda was already thinking about her next lesson plan and how she could make a deeper impact.

When questioned about this line of thinking, Melinda always retorted with a solid reply, "I have dreamt about becoming a teacher and instructing in this subject since I was a young girl. Until they tell me I cannot anymore, I am going to keep on doing the best job I possibly can do." And she did just that . . . for the next 23 years!

Suppose you ask to give a retirement speech about yourself. (In realizing this task would seem truly self-serving, please acknowledge it as a conversation starter.) What topics would be included in the speech? What outcomes would you have attained during the course of your tenure that would need to be mentioned? Who would be in the audience? What would you want them to say about you?

As we begin to think about hope, we must also consider our legacy and the rationale behind our decision to become a teacher in the first place. Needless to mention, those who have a plan and action steps usually find a clearer path to a desired result. Yet, as educators, our professional development is brimming with data meetings and assessment breakdowns, but rarely are we able to utilize this time to secure who we are in the system and what our impact will be via setting a goal.

There are many teachers like Melinda's colleagues who lose faith in the system. Thirty years is quite a long time for a person to stay engaged, especially when there are those who may not always see the value in who we are and what we do for students.

Did you ever wonder what happened to those grizzled veterans? How could people be so negative? Were these folks negative when they were hired or did something happen? When asked, many will state that they started out their careers with the same luster as the new folks, but somewhere along the line, the system caught up to them.

Maybe it was a series of ineffective administrators or central office personnel. Perhaps the kids changed over time. Or maybe life outside of school wore down the fabric of their spirit. Whatever the reasons, the gleam that once was has been dimmed.

Can you recall the reasons you wanted to be a teacher? Where were you when you made that decision? What were you feeling at the time? Reflective questioning takes us back to a time when the excitement about our decisions was overflowing.

Despite our individual stories, the common thread that connected all of our accounts had to do with hope. Somewhere within the framework of building a vision for our careers, we "believed" we could truly make a difference. In difficult times that sustain, that initial push lessens in intensity. But as teachers, we can never, ever let the light succumb to doubt.

We can wish to win the lottery any day of the week and twice on Sundays, but we can only ever hope to win the lottery after we have purchased a ticket!

For hope comes with a burden. Hope requires a yielding to things that we cannot control while promoting the ideals and mission that we can impact. Wishes cannot fail; but hope can, and that is what makes it so special a gift, so cherished a lifeline.

It is stated time and time again that teachers are the hope for the future. This is a fact! It is within the capacity and spirit of our teachers that we can inspire generations to move forward, to grow, and to hope.

PRACTICAL ADVICE

Assume good intentions until proven otherwise; then forgive.

Harboring negativity is bad for the mind, body, and soul. If you believe you have been wronged, talk about it. Find the facts and break through the assumptions. And if the proof supports the wrongdoing, find it in yourself to forgive. Life is too short wasted on petty grievances, especially when we have lives to impact . . . starting with our own.

Remember your why!

Recalling the reasons you wanted to become a teacher and finding ways to continually involve these principles will assist you in sustaining your stride. Remember, despair seeks the unfulfilled heart. Linking your passions, your person, to what you do will help to create a sense of purpose for you and your students.

FOR THE CLASSROOM

Utilize service-learning opportunities.

Finding purpose beyond the lesson assists students in connecting to a deeper meaning. When teachers create inspirational learning opportunities, and marry them with a moral purpose, the outcomes ascend all levels of learning.

Buy your ticket; help students buy theirs.

Magical moments in classroom dynamics occur daily. Our ability to inspire a student to stretch beyond what he thought was possible adds to the development of the whole child. Remember, ideas we hope for can fail; in knowing that, building our resilience and grit will help us weather lagging motivation.

The greatest gift we can bestow upon our students is to teach them to believe.

VIII

Manners and Methods

PROOF IS IN THE PUDDING.

TWENTY-ONE

Try It

A "Try It" is a curt, practical idea that a teacher can use immediately. A "Try It" ranges from concise strategies for success with people to simple actions to take in the classroom.

TRY IT: BUILD YOUR LEGACY FROM DAY ONE

Can you recall your favorite teacher? What was his or her name? Why do you consider him or her to be your favorite?

We all have had a Mrs. Millachap who has had a tremendous influence on our lives. Yet, what we remember about her is not necessarily the day-to-day details but the affective impression that she made upon us. In other words, we may not be able to evoke the 25th lesson that was taught, but we remember *how* she taught and the personal connection she made with us and our classmates.

There is an enormous difference between being "a" teacher and being "the" teacher for our students. "A" teacher is the type of person who blends into the others. There was nothing substantial or special about their teaching practice or the way that they interacted with students. As time passes, their name vanishes from existence like an old-fashioned eraser sweeping snowy chalk from the blackboard.

On the other hand, "the" teacher is the type of person that sustains no matter how much time has lapsed. The reasons she lives on is because she genuinely cared about the subject, but more so about each student. She smiled, was organized, and challenged thinking. Whatever the situation, her impact went beyond the tasks of the topic. She touched our minds and our hearts simultaneously.

Backwards design can be used in various aspects of life. When considering your legacy, be sure to plan with "the" in mind. Be the teacher whom your students will remember forever . . . and for positive reasons. Thanks, Mrs. M.

TRY IT: PROPOSE POSSIBLE SOLUTIONS

Harvey was the type of husband who wives "chat" about during book club nights. One of Harvey's favorite hobbies was to point out everything that was wrong with the house, the car, the kids, the neighbors, and so forth. His days consisted of finding fault with others, thus raising his own self-worth. In fact, he used to say that he enjoyed being the devil's advocate, and when someone would try to tell him he was being "that guy," he would always retort with, "Someone has to be."

Millie, Harvey's wife, was a lovely woman who was unfortunately married to a complainer. And the constant barrage of criticisms was wearing her down. She had dreamed for a day when, instead of telling her the doorknob was loose, Harvey would grab a screwdriver and fix it. Unfortunately, that was not in his nature. He certainly was "that guy."

Know anyone like Harvey in your school? Folks who repetitively find fault with situations without thinking through ways to fix them end up being labeled as complainers, negative, or worse.

There is nothing perfect about situations where adults must exist within the framework of a system that services children. Likewise, buildings, equipment, and goods also share the brunt of constant usage. Instead of being "that guy," look for ways to fix situations. If you must point out a problem prior to its resolution, be sure to also present a few possible solutions, especially to administrators who hear complaints all day long.

People can tolerate the devil's advocate only so much before they detach themselves from his presence. Good luck.

TRY IT: NO SURPRISES FOR ADMINISTRATORS

Surprises can be great! Birthdays, special anniversaries, or the occasional "just because" note can turn an ordinary day into a very special one. Yet, despite these grand occurrences, surprises can also be negative.

For example, think about when you take your car into the shop for its annual inspection. You say to yourself, "The car is running fine; got the oil changed last month. All should be good." No sooner do you leave the garage than you inevitably get that dreaded phone call from your mechanic. Surprise! You need brakes. Yikes!

These types of surprises we also remember, but not necessarily in the fondest manner. When dealing with your principal, it is best to avoid these surprise situations. A wise mentor teacher once said, "Bad news early and often." This was not to say that our days are compiled of negative experiences. On the contrary, teaching brings with it a host of positives from dawn to dusk. However, on those rare occasions when you feel something is array, it is best to give your principal a heads up.

Do not ever think that you are bothering your principal with this type of information. (And if she acts like you are, shame on her.) Better to disclose potential problematic situations than to allow her to be blind-sided by a student, parent, or another colleague. Remember, if it feels wrong, chances are it is.

This advice also serves as a guide for dealing with folks other than the principal. Do not hold onto bad news. Use the FYI to CYA. Keep us all on the same page and limit the surprises to birthdays and the like.

TRY IT: PLAY HOME GAMES

Ask the opponents of the Green Bay Packers if they enjoy getting ready to play a game on the frozen tundra of Lambeau Field or if visiting teams appreciate doing battle with the Boston Celtics at the Garden? Probably not! Home field advantage has its rewards.

If you are going to work in a school, you have to learn to deal with emotion. From the students and parents to the administrators and coun-selors, dealing with children brings out the best and worst in us. People can be ecstatic about certain situations and quite the opposite about oth-ers. In those times, try to play home games.

Home games in schools are situations that are generated by us. Meet-ings, phone calls, and the like, become home games when we set the appointment and guide the agenda. For example, if a parent calls fuming about an issue, do not take the call until you have gathered all of the facts about the situation. Once you have the information, call the parent back. (Try to call parents at their work because they are less likely to behave poorly there. Sly but true.)

It is understood that as a teacher, you may not have control over every situation when contact needs to be made. In those instances where you must meet with families or others who are upset, be sure to listen, empa-thize, and speak slowly.

Home breeds familiarity. Do not allow yourself to get caught off guard. No surprises! As the Packers at Lambeau, when we play a home game, the outcomes are more fortunate. I would love to see someone do a "Lambeau Leap" after a great parent conference. Wouldn't you?

TRY IT: FRONT PAGE MENTALITY

Parent Louella Golds was disappointed with her daughter. Tina, having watched TV instead of studying for her math quiz, glanced at someone else's paper and was now seated in the principal's office. Upset but composed, Mrs. Golds explained to her daughter the lesson of Front Page Mentality:

When dealing with difficult decisions, we must consider Front Page Mentality. In other words, what if the decision you were about to make landed on the front page of the newspaper? Would you be proud of your actions if your teacher, father, or mother saw it? If the answer is no, then make a different decision."

Obviously, the message rang loud and clear. Tina recovered from this event, partly because she was a great kid and partly because of the superb parenting that accompanied her journey.

What if your next decision was going to go viral? Seem absurd? It is not, especially in an age of instant stardom. There is an old saying that goes something like this—It is easy to be known for negative actions. It is quite astonishing to become famous for doing the right thing.

Although not glamorous, the moral action does not necessarily lead to an exterior pot of gold, and yet, the winnings of a solid and safe decision live on well past the wealth. When faced with a difficult decision, think about Mrs. Gold's simple rule. Picture yourself on the front page of your local newspaper with the caption underneath that recalls your last decision. You okay with it? If not, you know what to do.

Remember, as teachers, we are *ALWAYS* on!

TRY IT: NEVER GO "OFF THE RECORD"

There is no "off the record." Period. Just like the Miranda Warning, "anything you say can and will be held against you." This notice is not meant to scare anyone only to document that the "informal" in our profession does not exist.

For example, suppose you were complaining to the cafeteria ladies concerning the principal's inability to organize. Now let us consider that one of the ladies, who felt very uncomfortable about your rant, went to the principal to clear her name. In clearing her name, we must realize that she incriminated yours. Now, let's suppose your principal asks you about the situation. Are you going to tell him the truth? Lie? Plead the fifth?

If one thinks this type of situation does not occur in a school, please think again. People "clear" their names all the time. And many a person has been placed in a terrible position with other staff members because of going "off the record."

As a rule of thumb, if you cannot say what you are about to say to someone's face, then don't say it. To think that we garner immunity when we say "this is off the record" is foolish. If you must complain, find someone far away to listen. This way, you will not put yourself or the person in jeopardy.

In addition, if someone asks you to go off the record, politely tell him that you do not do that. If your opinion is really warranted, you should be able to say what you need to say regardless of the context. This especially goes for speaking with families or students as well.

We can think whatever we wish, but when we say it, we own it. Be smart.

TRY IT: THE TALK OUT

When people are very upset about a given situation, most times, they will want to be heard. In trying to be responsive to their needs, we sometimes try to "fix" the problem without first allowing the person to totally explain the situation.

One of the best practices we can employ is to be an active listener. Instead of trying to give input, allow the person to talk out. Take an interested position; take notes. And really try to hear what is being said. This way, you allow the person to exhaust the emotion involved with a dicey situation.

Plus, in a logical manner, listening makes sense. Think about it. In a potential difficult confrontation, we already know what we know. In other words, we do not have to research how we feel, what our opinion is. Yet, the information that is critical to realize before we react is what the other person knows. Think of it as playing a game of cards. Without knowing your opponent's hand, we are left in the blind to react and guess.

One of the best ways to locate another person's opinion is to allow them to tell us. However, our emotions sometimes push us to rectify the problem to bring us back to a balanced state. Remember, time is on our side in these situations. Use it to place yourself in a better position to find the win-win.

Admittedly, when a person is attacking the school, the staff, or you personally, it is difficult to keep your cool. However, as stated time and time again, always be pro. Stay focused on the end game. That's the sure play.

TRY IT: BE A PROACTIVE COMMUNICATOR

In an age of wondrous technology, there should be no reason why we are not proactive in our communication with families and students. We must see it as our professional responsibility to keep our students and parents actively engaged in our classroom. To do this to its most effective level, keeping everyone on the same page is a must!

Have a website. Post your assignments and test dates. Send e-mails, newsletters, notes. If you are still a person who writes the week's agenda on the board, snap a picture of it on your phone and e-mail that attachment to your families. Blog, tweet, and use ever necessary medium to keep your people informed.

As an aside, those who believe that we are teaching children responsibility when we do not take a proactive stance on allowing them access to information are just plain silly. Should we keep your checkbook balance a secret after you have seen it once on a screen? Please. Too often, what we think builds responsibility just builds frustration and *is not* in accord with the real world.

Being proactive might be a bit more work, but better to place the effort on the preemptive end then to try to explain in your next 504 meeting the reasons behind your personal responsibility experiment.

Knock the nonsense off and post your work.

PS . . . do you know your checking account balance right now?

TRY IT: DOCUMENT YOUR ACTIONS; HAVE A WITNESS

Have you even been caught in the middle of a "He said; she said" hullabaloo? If you were, chances are it took substantial time out of your day only to have your justifications rendered null and void by the other person's reasons.

One of the first ways to secure your position in a situation like this is to document your actions. Simply keeping a record of your phone calls, conversations and actions when it comes to potentially difficult scenarios will not only assist you, but also provide a basis for judgment. And please note your record does not have to be lengthy; record the facts and keep your opinions to yourself. Some find using bullet points in a chronological series to be best. Whatever you use, just be sure that it is accurate and devoid of estimation.

Unfortunately, no matter how accurate you take and present your notes, the standard "that's your opinion" will always be a viable option to refute your points.

There are going to be times in this job when people are going to disagree with your account of a specific event. *Nothing justifies the facts more than a witness's account.*

In heading into difficult parent meetings, challenging administrative consultations, and the like, make it part of your practice to have a witness in these types of situation.

The witness can be a union representative, colleague, counselor, or someone else not directly involved in the situation. Ask this person to take notes and be a great listener. This way, if the time ever comes to review the situation, this person will be able to present a unbiased interpretation of the event.

These may seem like no brainers, and in fact, they are! Document and whenever possible, secure a witness.

TRY IT: BE EARLY!

To arrive on time is to arrive late. And in the words of Forrest Gump, "That's all I'm going to say about that." Well, maybe a little more . . .

We are all busy bees. We all have a zillion and one items we need to attend to during the course of a given day. Nothing says "I appreciate you" more than to be early to meetings. However, it is amazing how many folks fail to realize this simple platitude.

Recall a time when you were expecting a meeting to start on time, and it was delayed because of someone else's tardiness. Now, we are human beings, and forgiveness is one of our greatest virtues, yet when people are habitually late, that action sends a negative message to all. No one's time is more important than another's.

There have been many incredible classroom teachers who have scarred their reputation because of actions outside of the classroom. Aside from the obvious offenses (crimes, negligent behavior, and so forth), one surefire way to lose credibility with colleagues is to be a Late Lucy. Once labeled as such, it is almost impossible to regain one's reputation. So set your clock ten minutes early or have a friend call you. Do whatever is necessary to assist yourself.

Lateness breeds a lack of professionalism and disregard for collaboration and congenial relationships. Period. Be early. And if you have to be late, please tell someone in advance if possible.

Be where you are supposed to be when you are supposed to be.

TRY IT: VALUE WAIT TIME

One of the most underappreciated tools in a teacher's toolbox is wait time. Wait time is the time that elapses when a student is attempting to answer a question. Now, some folks believe the time in between the question and the answer serves as a buffer to dialogue. Yet, perhaps if we could view wait time as part of the "unseen" personal dialogue, then maybe its value would be more appreciated in educational settings.

For example, our brains, as we discussed previously, look to make connections. These "brain conversations" occur instantaneously as students process questions and look to secure reasonable responses from the millions of informational pieces stored in their brains. The more divergent the question, the more possibilities exist in responding to it. In other words, the better we are at asking higher-level questions, the more time we should allow for thoughtful inner dialogue to occur.

Highly active, highly participatory lessons require thinking from all members of the classroom. In designing quality instruction, do not forget to include the bridge to stimulating illuminations. Do not see the pause as a symbol of weakness; see it as a statement of determination and a natural occurrence when we ask our students to stretch beyond lower-level questions.

All good things in time.

TWENTY-TWO

Don't Try It

A "Don't Try It" is the opposite of a "Try It." A "Don't Try It" is decision that should not be made by teachers for it often causes dissatisfaction with staff, students, families, and ultimately, oneself.

DON'T TRY IT: JOKES IN POWER

Just as there are ideas to try, there are also some you should avoid at all costs. One such suggestion has to do with "trying" to be funny. We all know the type—the teacher who loves to give his colleagues or students a dig—meant as "good clean fun." This teacher obviously does not know the difference between sarcasm and humor.

Perhaps this teacher was bullied on the playground, and now he sees this as his chance to conquer those ill feelings. Or perhaps he is just uncomfortable in social situations and needs to poke fun at someone to lighten the mood. Or perhaps he is just an ass!

Whatever the rationale, one thing is certain—he is going to crack a joke. And when he does, it's not going to be funny. Why? Because inevitably, someone is going to be hurt by his comments. Plus, these "comical" witticisms aimed at individuals erode the fabric of a positive climate, leading to an all-out assault on the culture.

Jokes in power are not jokes; they are reminders of who is in charge.

Even in situations where students or other colleagues may be prodding you to enter into a verbal skirmish, it is always best to remain professional instead of lowering yourself to the level of classroom bully.

Remember when mom used to say if you don't have something nice to say . . . ? Well, take that little nugget and carry it with you. Avoid the

117

mixture of humor and rank, as the combination is as lethal as carbon monoxide and as silent a killer of classroom morale as well.

DON'T TRY IT: REWARDING ONE

During one of my undergraduate classes, my professor used the "apple" experiment to make a great point. To make a long story longer, she used to give a team midterm. At the start of the next class, she would present two groups (out of six) with apples and state how proud she was of their efforts. Without mentioning scores (or even handing back the tests), she would proceed with class as normal.

As break concluded, she would pass out the assessments. Inevitably, the class would soon figure out that the two lauded groups had scores similar to the entire class. Without fail, she would sit and wait for someone to ask, "Why did they get an apple and we did not?" And with that, she would start the lesson on motivation. (Nice job, Dr. D.)

Sparing you a dissertation on motivational research, know that people can sometimes be fragile (or "fra geel lee" if you are Darren McGavin fan) in our business. Rarely are individuals motivated by the rewards of others. Congratulating one as Student of the Month sends myriads of others into the hallway questioning their worth.

I am not saying that timely praise is unhealthy. Large group accomplishments can and should be shared as a team. However, for individual triumphs, chat with the student in private. Many a teacher has had the best of intentions when it comes to praising his/her class only to witness the floor crumble beneath their feet. Think fruit.

If you are going to give out apples, you had better buy a bushel.

DON'T TRY IT: BEING THEIR FRIEND

Friendly not friends. This maxim has guided many a teacher on the road to building successful relationships with her class. Unfortunately, not everyone follows such sound advice.

Regrettably, we have all been witness to tragic events where a teacher's lack of professionalism has been made public with decisions involving minors. Obviously, these offenses yield much higher consequences. Yet, more subtle instances of poor judgment tend to go unnoticed at first, but can lead to negative outcomes for classroom culture.

A teacher has the responsibility of keeping balance in his classroom. In a sense, we have to ensure that the rights of the individual and the rights of the collective are in harmony. In juggling this critical act, sometimes we will affirm people's needs, and sometimes we will need to say "no."

Just as a parent who bribes a child to go to bed with candy can create a covetous little one, so too we can create the illusion of compliance when we substitute an external motivation (in this case, a false rationale for action) for what should be internal (wanting to do it because it is right or even because we have to do so). Too much good can sometimes be a bad thing.

In looking for the win-win situation, one does not have to acquiesce to garner favor with others. It's okay to say "no" and mean it. Working hard to be liked is foolish. Work hard and people might like you for being organized, challenging, and humane. And if they do not, that is okay too.

Leadership by bartering only serves to build false expectation.

DON'T TRY IT: THE GENERAL WARNING

In walking the hallways in your school, have you ever heard this declaration come from a colleague to his or her class?

> *I am really getting tired of the teasing that is occurring in our room. We talked about this last week and the week before. Everyone in our classroom is valued, and we need to be mindful of our words. I am asking you again to be respectful of one another and to do your best to treat people as you would want to be treated.*

How do you feel after reading this statement? Now imagine how the students feel. The teacher had addressed the issue several times previously and instead of having the personal conversation (and more difficult one) with the students responsible for the teasing, he opted to use a general warning . . . again.

Look—most times it is fairly easy to figure out who did what to whom. Too often, we hide behind the general warnings when best practice would be to hold one-on-one conferences to get to the bottom of the issue. And if students are still making poor decisions, let them know. Define the expectations with respect, dignity, and a smidgen of firmness. Also, be sure to contact the parents. Teachers who duck parent calls often end up worse for the wear.

As stated before, teachers need to keep the balance. Please, please, please do not take the easy way out. Better to be a little uncomfortable now than to try to fix a culture that is stained by our inability to do the tough work.

DON'T TRY IT: DON'T UNDERESTIMATE THE QUIET CHILD

We have all heard the saying "the squeaky wheel gets the oil." Now, however true this statement may be, this philosophy should not be practiced when it comes to building effective learning environments.

We all have probably had some experience with a classroom brain—the type of child who has the answers before the questions are even asked. Admittedly, it is difficult not to rely on her, especially when the conversations start to wane. And although we witness this child's hand constantly in the air, what we may not see is the quiet child's purposeful pondering.

Obviously, classroom participation is critically important, and students should be encouraged to be active members of the learning community. However, some students are just quiet by nature. Previously, these students were thought not to be of the same ilk as more active students; yet, with the recent brain research, we are starting to realize that the personal conversations are just as important in the learning process as the vocalized ones.

There are various reasons for a student to be more verbal than another. But volume does not constitute IQ—and frequency does not necessitate achievement. Quiet students are not slow; they are just quiet. Assisting these students to become more verbal is okay, but forcing them to be may have negative consequences. Balance.

DON'T TRY IT: GIVE THE RIDICULOUS CREDENCE

Whenever the Brenda Barnes of the world (the school's gossip queen) starts to spout off about the latest central office conspiracy theory, the best bet is to reject the ridiculous as truth.

We all have been warned about the dangers of gossip, yet we sometimes fail to realize that our approval or dismissal of said gossip not only extends or diminishes the lie, it also places value on our person. In other words, when we agree with the absurd, we minimize our credibility with others who have withheld judgment. In a sense, our agreement with such statements, when they are devoid of fact, places us in alignment with the Brendas of the building.

For example, if Brenda was in a group of people stating that the latest technology initiative (giving everyone a laptop) was a way to spy upon teachers' free time, and you happen to just nod your head (not so much in agreement, but to be dismissive of her claim), others may think you agree with her. As the story is retold, guess whose name starts to enter the conspiracy team?

Sticks and stones, as the saying goes, wound the will. We must be vigilant when it comes to others' search for acceptance by promoting untruths. We cannot get sucked into their attention grabs by our innocent treaties. If someone is gossiping, we must ask for facts. We must also be brave enough to render a decision on the situation. In simple terms, if you think the story is bogus, it is okay to say it with respect.

And if you are not the type of person who can stomach calling the gossiper out, perhaps avoidance of this person may be the best plan of attack.

DON'T TRY IT: BE WARY OF PERSONAL PATTERNS

Habits bring familiarity; familiarity brings comfort. And for teachers, routines are a mainstay in organized and effective classrooms. However, sometimes the patterns that we evoke may have unintended negative consequences, and unless corrected, could limit achievement potential.

First, we must be aware of our speech patterns. In a profession where much depends upon what we say, we must be mindful of the manner in which we are speaking. For example, sometimes we develop verbal "helpers" to tell the listener when we are about to disagree with them or perhaps present something controversial. When we use starters like "quite honestly," we are telling the people that perhaps we have not been honest in prior conversations. As teachers, we need to examine our speech patterns to hear what we are "saying" to people (whether we mean it or not).

Furthermore, if you are right-handed, chances are that you talk to the right side of the room more often than the left. This is not to say that those on the left deserve less attention; it's just a tendency that exists when it comes to public speaking and comfort. Do your best to vary your proximity. Make the left the right and vice versa. In this manner, all of your students will feel like you are making a personal connection to them.

Look for ways to communicate your thoughts without using personal crutches.

DON'T TRY IT: HINTING AT CONFIDENTIAL MATTERS

It is funny how often we learn something in grade school and it becomes a life lesson. Remember that childhood chant, "I know something, but I won't tell." Remember what your teacher would say when someone was singing it? Chances are, it was not a pleasurable response. But why?

When people hint at confidential matters, they create a sense of power for themselves (I know something) while also creating a feeling of help-lessness for the listener (but I won't tell). Most times, the information (critical or not) is presented as an imperative—serving to heighten anxiety and create a power imbalance (I *won't* tell).

People in perceived positions of power (having information) play this little game all the time. Whether purposeful ("I wish I could tell you about the Smalls' situation.") or not ("My day is crazy busy; got this huge 504 to handle."), these types of comments create an imbalance of the haves and have-nots.

If you are working on something you know you cannot talk about, then don't talk about it. Hinting about it without a clear explanation creates ill feelings. Likewise, when someone asks us how our day is going, we may be "very busy," but to imply that we are busier than the people around us again produces the divide in the team. "My day is pretty hectic, as I am sure yours is teaching students how to read." Simple tags to the original line may serve to foster a greater sense of togetherness.

Secure your statue by performing your job with humility and dignity. Do not undermine your (or someone else's) efforts by relying on tactical measures of attention gaining. If you cannot tell, don't even start in the first place.

DON'T TRY IT: SAY YOU CAN WHEN YOU CANNOT

There are those who insist they do not care what folks think about them. These supposed "lone wolves" pride themselves on being isolated from peer pressure and acceptance issues. However, we must ask ourselves critical questions when it comes to our profession: what type of people usually become teachers?

Of the multitude of traits that we possess, one quality that many of us demonstrate is the need for affirmation. Now, please do not look at this trait as a negative one, but as a possible statement of truth. In simple terms, the amazing feeling that we sense when a student "gets it" drives us to present the next lesson. Being the type of "people pleasers" that we can be, sometimes we are placed into difficult situations that require us to say "no." One such instance happens when we are asked to champion causes or activities.

Many professionals have said "yes" to sponsoring an event only to either to back out at the last minute or complete the activity with a despondent attitude. Such actions hurt not only the students involved, but also the individual by placing him or her in a position of helplessness (for the time to take control has passed). Many of us do not enjoy being the bad cop. It's difficult, but oftentimes necessary when we are dealing with balancing power, resources, and the like.

Saying "no" is not an indictment on our character. If you cannot commit to doing something, then simply do not do it. But be honest as soon as possible. As the saying goes, "Pulling the bandage off fast. Better to sting for a moment, then for a longer time and at more intensity."

Remember, we do not build a positive legacy by being perceived as a person who cannot follow through with tasks. If you can, great. If not, just say it and move on.

DON'T TRY IT: POSTING YOUR GRADES LATE

Aside from health, welfare, and safety issues in schools, nothing upsets parents more than a teacher who is behind on posting grades. It truly is astonishing to witness. Truly great teachers, who work so hard in the classroom, lose their deserved reputations over an inability to stay ahead of their assignments. And these are the great teachers; imagine what folks think of the ones who are habitually late with grades.

Timing and grading deal with respect. We all understand that situations happen in our lives that can sometime hinder us from getting everything we want accomplished. However, in times of need, many would volunteer to assist. Likewise, parents are quick to forgive teachers for the occasional slip. But those who make it a habit of being behind convey disorganization and disregard for student well-being.

In addition, have you ever been in the supermarket, thought you had cash in your wallet, only to get to the register with a cart full of food and a wallet full of air? How did you feel? Embarrassed? A bit put off? Of course, you could always swipe the credit card, but the point has been made.

When we fail to report accurate grades, we sometimes "take the cash out of our students "wallet" by presenting a false reality. Do this a few times, and it is no wonder some of the students "stop shopping" in our class.

We all have a job to do, and one of the most important jobs for a teacher is to keep accurate student achievement marks. Make the time for grading and ask for assistance early if needed.

TWENTY-THREE

Case Studies

The following are situations that connect to each chapter. They are designed to spur conversation and look to examine the key points of each chapter. Often times, the case study is best when used prior to reading the chapter.

CASE STUDY 1—WHAT'S IN YOUR CUP?

Jennifer Scott dreaded the third Wednesday of every month. Although a very positive and energetic teacher, Jennifer became despondent during her social studies department meetings. Much of the reason for her downtrodden spirit had to do with her colleague, Del, and his incessant opinions.

Del was a very bright fellow, but not much for the humility. In fact, he was a "know-it-all." From his views on early civilizations to current world politics, Del had an opinion and was never at a loss for sharing his thoughts. Being a very smart fellow, he was also very skilled in arguing. This made for a very uncomfortable scene, especially for folks like Jennifer who preferred a more collegial approach.

If you were Jennifer, how could you handle this situation? Is there anything that can happen to make this a more collaborative team? What other folks might need to be involved in this situation?

Something to Consider

No one should have to endure another person's bullish behavior. If you are in a situation as described, you have every right to do something about it. Obviously, people may be uncomfortable addressing issues that they did not necessarily create; however, if you cannot withstand the barrage, you owe it to yourself and the team to take action.

CASE STUDY 2—PUT YOUR PASSION INTO ACTION

Vicki Cross is a very good teacher who has been a member of Hollow High School staff for almost two decades. Most days, she is as chipper as a clam; but lately, her demeanor has shifted. In a private conversation with you, she revealed that although she loves the students, she was starting to become bored with her subject.

Knowing she truly does not want to leave the ranks of the teaching profession, what advice would you give her? How can she find new life within the framework of her class? Try to give practical ideas (ones that can actually be accomplished).

Something to Consider

"What" we teach may be at the discretion of the state or the local district, but how and why we teach falls under our control. Looking for ways to bring passion into one's classroom can make all the difference. Likewise, employing a few new best-practice strategies can also give teachers that little charge when it comes to the everyday grind. The school year is long; best to utilize variety and fresh perspectives to stay positive and effective. Furthermore, taking classes can also help to boost morale by establishing a fresh perspective with new knowledge.

CASE STUDY 3—"WHAT TO DO WITH JOHNNY?"

Casey Jones is a middle school science teacher with a problem. Today in his last period of the day, Joey Vickers asked to leave his class early because he needed to get to his school football game. In being new to the school, Mr. Jones politely said "no" to Joey, for although the policy states that student-athletes can leave early for games, it also states that it is up to the teacher's discretion if leaving will hinder the student's grade. Joey reluctantly sat down.

Joey was twenty minutes late to the game. Being the starting quarterback, his teammates and coaches were visibly upset. Joey explained the situation to his coach, Mr. Broomall, who promised to speak to Mr. Jones first thing in the morning.

Which person is right in this situation? Is it okay for Mr. Jones to not allow Joey to leave early? Does Coach Broomall have a legitimate argument, considering his best player was not at the game (and not because of disciplinary reasons)?

Something to Consider

Tough call. Fair is not always equal, and both adults truly have valid arguments. The sure bet would be to follow the school/district policy when it deals with student athletes. Obviously, each could give a bit when it comes to their position; however, the priority of the school should ultimately dictate the "most correct" action. (On a personal note, I would allow students to go to their games. I felt that having other adults interested in their work added value. Again, this is not an easy decision.)

CASE STUDY 4—MY MIRACLE

"It's never the parents you need to see who make appointments for conferences." Mrs. Moody bellowed as she started back to her classroom to meet with Dr. Mallon about her daughter Theresa. Theresa was a straight-*A* student and the type of child most would be proud to have raised.

Mrs. Moody hurried through the standard format of the conference, pointing out the obvious strong points. She ended the meeting by stating if she needed to chat, Dr. Mallon, she knew where to find her.

The next morning, the principal asked to meet with Mrs. Moody in her office, as Dr. Mallon was not happy with yesterday's conference.

If you were the principal, what advice would you give to Mrs. Moody? Do students with great grades deserve a meeting? Talk about demeanor and delivery. How can we sustain a positive culture for all students?

Something to Consider

Mrs. Moody may not need to see Dr. Mallon, but she should want to see her and certainly should make Dr. Mallon feel valued. Just because students are doing well in class, does not mean that all is well or that they will continue to attain a high level unless the right feedback is given. Furthermore, we should want parents to be engaged with their child's schooling. There is nothing wrong with affirming a parent's efforts. We are here for all.

CASE STUDY 5—COUNTER MELODIES

What are the benefits of the following situations?

- A broken copier
- A full parking lot
- No coffee left in the pot
- The snack machine being out of order

Be sure to discuss your thinking and try to anticipate impacts on other human beings close to these items. What lessons can we draw from admiring the antithesis?

Something to Consider

The antithesis may serve as the driving force behind some of the most positive situations in our lives. We must appreciate these situations and hold tight to the premise that actions are; it is our reaction to them that support the affective nature of judgment. In simple terms, the counter melody can be beautiful alongside the main one or in and of itself. It is up to us to keep our value system open to all possibilities.

CASE STUDY 6—THE BUOYANCE TRIAL

In being an 11th grade American history teacher, Mr. Highland was required by the state to teach slavery; however, he knew he had three African American students in his class. One of those student's mother's was the head of the NAACP and had been in discussions before about the lack of diversity training in the district.

If you were Mr. Highland, what would you do? Who would you involve? Would you teach the lesson? If so, how? If not, is this decision good for all students?

Something to Consider

Remember, the why is so much more powerful than the what. If Mr. Highland takes a practical and positive approach to the topic, this may be a quality lesson for all students. We cannot assume something is wrong, and the best way to not assume it is to solicit the facts. Perhaps prior conversations with folks of color could really benefit Mr. Highland's perspective and teaching approach for all sorts of topics. Ask and we shall receive.

CASE STUDY 7 — CRITICAL CONNECTIONS — START WITH THE WHY!

Nelson Robbins is very upset about the new state assessment in civics. Although he agrees that there should be a standardized approach to the information about our government, the specific text documents and dates of interest that were selected by the state auditors do not mesh with his approach.

Knowing he will have to change many of his lessons and assessments, how could you assist him with this transition? How do you teach what is required but still create a thematic basis for your units?

Something to Consider

If students can locate the exact information on the Internet that connects to one's methodology of teaching, then that practice would probably be considered inadequate. In other words, the connection to "why" must guide the lesson, so that ideas and opinions are allowed to grow into solid arguments (with foundation and tangible support). Having students work through divergent thinking models, where choice is a mainstay, provides the necessary motivation to create dynamic learning. In other words, if Independence Day occurred on July 4, 1777, would it be less significant?

CASE STUDY 8 — "BEHIND THE CURTAIN" IS THE GOLD!

Lucy Fields was an amazing elementary school teacher who had a flare for instruction. In fact, she was the Winds Elementary go-to person. Whenever some needed a fresh idea for literary centers or close reading strategies, Lucy was the one.

During an afternoon professional development session, Lucy presented an idea of involving the students in your planning. In a nutshell, her vision was to include the students in the understanding "why" certain strategies were selected by the teacher to be utilized in the classroom. Lucy explained that "if students knew what a literary center was (and what the practice tried to accomplish with students), they would be more connected to the learning."

Teachers, though, did not have that same energy for Lucy's idea this time. People spoke about time commitments and the amount of work it would take to actually "teach kids how to teach." Her goal, along with the principal's, was for everyone to try this type of lesson by month's end.

How do you feel about this issue? Could teaching students how to teach improve their learning? How does knowledge of strategies increase motivation?

Something to Consider

We must consider the positive and negative consequences of change. Perhaps the very strategies that make some teachers highly effective could assist students in being more interested in their learning. In other words, we cannot dictate feeling; only present the facts and allow one's conscious to judge its worth.

CASE STUDY 9—PROVE IT!

Mrs. Jennings, mother to Marissa, was upset with Dorothy Smart, a sixth grade math teacher. Mrs. Jennings was distraught because her daughter received points off of her math assessment because she did not "show her work" on all of the problems. The dilemma for Mrs. Jennings was that Marissa got every answer correct.

Is it okay to take points off for not showing all of the work on an assignment? Should Marissa be permitted to show the work now? Retake the test? What is the life lesson connected to showing one's work? How would students show their work in your class? How would you answer a complaint about your procedures?

Something to Consider

We are teaching children how to fish. Securing the correct answer today does not constitute finding it tomorrow unless we have the necessary skills to do so. However, we must be proactive in communicating our rationale with students and families. Failure to do so could be misconstrued as being deceptive. In establishing lifelong learning, why not allow students to hand in assignments and assessments until they are correct? Do not worry about the grade; lead with the learning. That is why we are here!

CASE STUDY 10—THE CONVERSATION UPSTAIRS

Jackie Burns was a conscientious third grade teacher, but unfortunately, she was at her limit with Dr. Kent, the assistant principal of Wilkes Elementary School. During a recent data meeting, Dr. Kent was stressing the need to make decisions using the most recent data. Jackie, in feeling like

Dr. Kent was treating the team like children, rolled her eyes to one of her colleagues in the room.

Dr. Kent happened to notice Jackie's nonverbal action, and asked, "Ms. Burns, is there a problem?"

If you were Jackie, how would you handle this situation? Would you speak your truth in a public meeting? Talk about nonverbal clues to thinking? Should Jackie mind her P's and Q's next time?

Something to Consider

We must be mindful of the messages we are sending to others by both our nonverbal and our verbal responses to situations. Yet, if Jackie feels this way, someone else on the team may also feel like the team is being disrespected. But now is not the time to discuss this issue. Best to wait until a less volatile time and secure one's thinking instead of marching into an all-out assault on the boss.

In addition, please do not write anonymous letters. This type of workplace terrorist act does not garner the end result that people seek. Be honest and respectful, and people will reciprocate. If you cannot be honest with the boss, go to his boss, but do not send the message anonymously.

CASE STUDY 11 — "ALL I DO FOR THIS PLACE!"

Todd Stimbau was the math department chair in Elks High School. Unfortunately for Todd, there was a new principal, Dr. Varber, who was interested in moving the math department forward. Both Todd and Dr. Varber had met on several occasions with the math coordinator for the district to review different ideas, which ironically have come from a teacher committee.

Again, Todd was not interested in the changes or following suit with the "new guard" who seemed to be turning their backs on tradition. He stepped down from his position stating that after giving so much of himself over the past twenty-three years, he was not going to cooperate with a bureaucracy that would inevitable ruin the department.

Two days later, there was a new department head, Melanie Smith, and the teacher-lead initiatives were put into place.

How do you feel about this situation? Should Todd have stepped down? Should Melanie have stepped up? What assumption did Todd make concerning his status, the opinions of the department, and so forth? What lessons can be taken from this short vignette?

Something to Consider

When we assume higher self-worth in relation to the opinions of others, we place ourselves into a precarious position. Change is inevitable; our reaction to it defines our legacy. Locating the rationale for ourselves and others is paramount.

CASE STUDY 12 — "IT IS WHAT IT IS"

"Class size is just on the rise," said Ted Knowles, an experienced 10th grade business teacher. "And there's not a darn thing we can do about it."

Sarah Marks, a new teacher to Woodbine High, was silent during the conversation among the other members of the business department. Although the conversation was matter-of-fact, the tone definitely reflected a feeling of helplessness. Sarah knew she could not hire new staff to address the growing population; however, she did have a few instructional ideas that could assist with the numbers.

If you were Sarah, would you say anything? If so, what would it be? Do you have any instructional ideas that could help with rising class size? How will you stay positive when others are not? What is within your control?

Something to Consider

There are always strategies that can be utilized when class size is on the rise. Differentiated grouping, running centers, and staggered starts are just a few. The key is to stay positive no matter the situation. When we succumb to helplessness, we drag ourselves and others into a state of misery. We may not have control over the action, but we do have it over our optimism and the next actions we will take regarding the current situation.

CASE STUDY 13 — THE CONSPIRACY THEORIST

Reuben Waltz was an art teacher at East Elementary, and he was convinced that central office was ignoring his school. Whenever a situation would present itself (budget cuts, redistricting, etc.), Reuben would chatter about how he knew East was going to be a target.

In short, Reuben had always felt that Superintendent O'Ryan disliked him because he "never attended any of the art evenings at East." Although an enormous district, Reuben was convinced that Superintendent O'Ryan was deliberately ignoring East's accomplishments. Furthermore, whenever he had an opportunity, he made sure to let the folks on East's staff "know the truth" about these purposeful snubs by central office.

Aside from the size of the district, can you cite other reasons for the Superintendent's absence? If you can, what does this say about Reuben's premise? If you were Reuben, what would you do? How does Reuben's opinion impact the other staff members, central office, and the culture of East? Does Reuben gain from these situations?

Something to Consider

Conspiracies start when we decisively decide not to investigate the facts. Likewise, the continual assault on a "perceived" enemy only promotes ill will and a feeling of helplessness on behalf of the listeners. Preventing the efforts of the conspirator may be an uneasy proposition, but one that is warranted to assist a healthy culture and climate.

CASE STUDY 14—THE CLOSER THE BETTER

Mrs. Christie, a seventh grade social studies teacher, was very upset with Coach Kline's decision to allow Mike Bow to play in his seventh grade hockey game. In fact, she was so upset that she made a formal complaint to the assistant principal.

Mrs. Christie believed that Mike should be held accountable for his "antics" in her classroom. In writing several office referrals, she was convinced that students who had been given office consequences were banned from games that day (although she could not find this statement in the discipline code). On the other hand, Coach Kline felt that Mrs. Christie was being ridiculous. Known for having questionable classroom management strategies, Mrs. Christie was not garnering Kline's support.

If you were the assistant principal, what would you do? What steps would you take to solve this issue? How would you define the win? What advice would you give to both parties?

Something to Consider

Win-win situations seem to be a mainstay in settling various disputes involving opponents. But why? Perhaps the reason stems from the fact that human beings rarely exist in direct opposition when dealing with human issues. In other words, unless both can agree upon a defined outcome (in definition and action), we must come to realize that each position can indeed succeed or fail based upon the specific lens we select in viewing the argument.

CASE STUDY 15—DON'T BITE THE BOSS

Terry Misler was really upset with her new principal, Stuart Jackson. Terry, who was a tenth grade reading specialist, had made a decision to schedule *a* few proficient students into her class this quarter in the hopes of sustaining their growth. Coming as a surprise to him, Mr. Jackson asked to meet with Terry.

Although Mr. Jackson agreed with the move, he had told Terry he wished she had come to him first and also stated he would like to see the data that was used to make such a determination. Terry was quiet during the meeting; she was not used to principals who meddled in the day-to-day decisions of teachers.

Back in the team room, Terry erupted to her colleagues about her meeting with Mr. Jackson, the incompetence and lack of respect he had demonstrated by questioning her judgment about a job she "had been doing long before his birth."

Two days later, Terry got a message to meet with Mr. Jackson in his office at 3 p.m. to discuss her concerns with his management style.

If you were Terry, how would you handle this meeting? What would you say? How did Mr. Jackson know Terry was upset? Where can Terry go from here?

Something to Consider

Blasting the boss is ill advised. Even though we may feel upset with a given situation pertaining to the boss, we have to refrain from public floggings. If you cannot respect the person, at least respect the position.

CASE STUDY 16—"SAY IT AIN'T SO, JOE."

Marybeth Walker was a new middle school math teacher and committed to doing things "the correct way." Marybeth followed the notion that if one was going to assign homework, it is best practice to review it instead of just grading for completion. In sharing this premise with the families on Back to School Night, many applauded Marybeth for this practice. However, the accolades were very short-lived.

In staying with her plan, Marybeth took the time to review each problem to the fullest extent; however, this left little time for new instruction and follow-up. In following a scripted program, Marybeth was apprehensive about reducing the number of problems given each night.

By the third week, the principal's phone was ringing off the hook for students to be taken out of her class.

If you were Marybeth, what would you do? If skipping homework were not an option, would you go back on your premise? What would this say to families? How does this scenario speak to pressures on teachers?

Something to Consider

One must identify which variables are stagnant and which ones can be manipulated. Sometimes doing something the correct way may not be the right way, depending on the outcome of the practice.

CASE STUDY 17—WHAT'S THE WIN?

Imagine you are part of a team of English teachers instructing the honors classes. The principal has asked for recommendations for supplemental reading instruction for students who are struggling. One of your teammates believes you should use program A; another is opposed insisting on program Z. Neither is willing to budge.

Knowing each day that goes by is another day of lost instruction for struggling students, what actions could you take to assist with this outcome? What is winning in this situation? What folks would you involve in this situation? (Please assume that neither program can be split. In other words, one must be selected to be used with authenticity.)

Something to Consider

Wins need to be defined as situations where students receive what they need. If everyone is in agreement for the support, the adults must look past the adult issues and focus upon what is best for the children—in this case, securing extra literacy instruction. Both programs (and their faults) are better than nothing.

CASE STUDY 18—COMPARED TO WHAT

Gloria Sands was a quality instructor. She was well respected by her colleagues, and for the most part, families and students felt the same. Yet,

Bob Fellows, an eighth grade student in her class, did not feel so satisfied with Gloria's methods. In fact, he really disliked her.

On this particular day, Bob decided he had had enough of Gloria's class and walked out. As he was leaving, Gloria asked what the problem was, and with that, Bob told her (and the class) that she was "the worst teacher" he had ever experienced.

Following protocol, Gloria turned in the proper paperwork to the office, and Bob received his punishment that Friday. However, over the weekend, Gloria could not help but to question her worth? Was she "the worst?" Bob was really successful in other classes, yet, he struggled in hers. Was there something she was doing to trigger this behavior?

If you were Gloria, what would your next steps be? Obviously, a conversation with Bob would be appropriate, but what would you do after that? Conversely, what if you felt Bob's outburst was completely unprovoked. On what grounds could you make that assertion? In other words, what data would support your argument? Do great scores always produce "great" teachers behind them?

Something to Consider

Proof is relative to the issue. What sets standards is our ability to define agreeable outcomes and build consensus for actions. Before we can determine if Gloria is the worst, we must first understand what *worst* means to Bob, Gloria, the situation, and so forth.

CASE STUDY 19—13.1

Victor Hues was completing his preconference sheet for his principal. Of the many questions that intrigued him, the following two stood out: How do you define success in your classroom? What are the measures you utilize for proving a child has been successful in their experience with you?

Victor realized the questions were alluding to assessment scores; and of course, Victor saw the value of such. However, he could not help but feel like we were missing the boat on other humanistic goals. "Should not student success be tied to who a person is instead of what they can do?"

Do you agree or disagree with Victor? Please select a position and defend it. Are schools creating students who must win at all costs? Is there no place to instruct on character education and self-esteem amidst the standardized assessment barrage?

Something to Consider

Those who consistently tie success to the outcome of an action inherently create issues for children who are trying to learn the material and also who they are. We must work to balance the scores with personal initiatives. Just as current standardized assessment rewards growth, we must also look to encourage trial and error in relation to attaining high scores. Potential exists in both scholastic and social pursuits. Cultivate for all.

CASE STUDY 20 — THE BURDEN OF HOPE

Joel was not opposed to having a mentor. In being a new ninth grade science teacher, he knew he was not an expert. However, Joel's growing contempt for the mentorship program had less to do with the program itself, but more to do with his mentor, Harold.

Harold was an experienced teacher, but for all purposes, a miserable man. Joel could not understand how Harold was selected to be a mentor. He did his best to avoid contact with him, but inevitably, this tactic could only suffice for so long, as non-tenure tasks needed to be completed. Unfortunately, the time with Harold was starting to really impact Joel's attitude and mindset. How could someone who is so miserable be working with students?

If you were Joel, what would you do? Whom would you talk to? What happens to grizzled veterans? What causes such disdain for the profession? How will you fight against becoming a Harold?

Something to Consider

Remember, there is no greater gift to bestow upon our students than the strength to believe. In striving to install a "can do" attitude in our children, we must also model the same positive spirit we seek in them. In understanding that failures occur, it is the resilient person who continues to hope despite whatever misfortune has befallen them. In addition, age does not dictate mindset. We control our thinking; the first step in deciding not to be miserable is to decide.

IX

Summation

PLAN WITH YOUR BRAIN; PROVE WITH YOUR HEART.

TWENTY-FOUR
Summary

Thank you for your purchase of this text. I hope you have found it to be helpful in your quest to be "the" teacher for your students and colleagues. Of all of the useful information that you have hopefully gathered while reading, perhaps the summation's quote best defines the journey:

Plan with your brain; prove with your heart.

One of our primary responsibilities is to shape the minds of our students. In approaching this work, it can sometimes become too easy to focus upon only intellectual goals, noting that such a quest can certainly bring us to some of the highest pinnacles of scholarship.

However, despite this worthy pursuit, we must always remember we work with human beings. And our ability to balance the academic plans with a healthy dose of the affective will ultimately assist us in this mission.

Remember, it is difficult to instruct a child who we do not know. Take the risk involved with personalizing the education for every student. Be "the" teacher your students will talk about for years to come. Do it because they bring value to them, not necessarily to you. These are the seeds of a successful career.

Never underestimate the influence.

All the Best
— *Tony*

Bibliography

Baum, F. (1900). *The wonderful Wizard of Oz*. Chicago, IL: George M. Hill Company.

Clabaugh, K. G., & Rozycki, G. E. (1990). *Understanding schools: The foundations of education*. New York: Harper and Row.

Fienberg, W., & Soltis, J. F. (1998). *School and society*. New York: Teachers College Press.

Goleman, D. (1995). *Emotional intelligence: Why it can matter more than IQ*. New York: Bantam.

Gropman, D. (1979). *Say it ain't so, Joe!: The true story of Shoeless Joe Jackson*. New York: Kensington Publishing Corporation.

Hobart, P. (2003). *Kishido: The way of the Western warrior*. Prescott, AZ: Hohm Press.

Knowles, M. (1984). *Andragogy in action: Applying modern principles of adult learning*. San Francisco, CA: Jossey-Bass.

Kuhlthau, C., Maniotes, L., & Caspari, A. (2007). *Guided inquiry: Learning in the 21st century*. Westport, CT: Libraries Unlimited.

Rios, F. A., & C. R. Stanton (2011). *Understanding multicultural education: Equity for all students*. Lanham, MD: Rowman and Littlefield Education.

Tzu, S. (1910). *The art of war*. (L. Giles, Trans.). London: Department of Oriental Printed Books and MSS in the British Museum.

Williams, J. (1981). *Indiana Jones: The soundtracks collection*. Columbia Records.

Willie, C. V. (1983). *Race, ethnicity and socioeconomic status: A theoretical analysis of their interrelationship*. Lanham, MD: Rowman and Littlefield.